T0294400

Early Automobiles

A History in Advertising Line Art, 1890-1930

The Electrobat (1895), America's first successful electric automobile.

Largely forgotten, the Electrobat was America's first successful electric automobile. A collaboration between mechanical engineer Henry G. Morris and chemist Pedro G. Salom, it was built in Philadelphia. Previously, both men had been involved with battery-powered streetcars. Building a prototype vehicle, they received a patent on August 31, 1894. Commercial production began in 1895. Their enterprise became the Morris & Salom Electric Carriage & Wagon Co. in 1896. An Electrobat was entered in America's first official horseless carriage race, Chicago's *Times-Herald* competition of Nov. 28, 1895. Unfortunately, icy road conditions prevented it from finishing the race, which was won by a gas-powered Duryea. The Electrobat used in that event was a two-passenger runabout. It had 40-inch diameter wheels in front, and 28-inch in the rear. Powered by two 1.5-hp Lundell motors, its driving gears were attached to the front axle. In good conditions on a smooth road it could reach speeds of 20 mph. On September 7, 1896 an Electrobat did much better, placing second, ahead of five Duryea vehicles, in the Narragansett Park Race held during Rhode Island's State Fair. Electrobat manufacture ceased in 1897, as the company shifted production to electric-powered hansom cabs.

Early Automobiles

A History in Advertising Line Art, 1890-1930

Jim Harter

WingsPress

San Antonio, Texas
2015

Early Automobiles: A History in Advertising Line Art, 1890-1930
© 2015 by Wings Press for Jim Harter

First Edition

Print Edition ISBN: 978-1-60940-489-5
ePub ISBN: 978-1-60940-490-1
Kindle ISBN: 978-1-60940-491-8
Library PDF ISBN: 978-1-60940-492-5

Wings Press
627 E. Guenther
San Antonio, Texas 78210
Phone/fax: (210) 271-7805

On-line catalogue and ordering:
www.wingspress.com
All Wings Press titles are distributed to the trade by
Independent Publishers Group
www.ipgbook.com

Library of Congress Cataloging-in-Publication Data:

Harter, Jim.
  Early automobiles : a history in advertising line art, 1890-1930 / Jim Harter. -- First edition.
     pages cm
  Includes bibliographical references and index.
   ISBN 978-1-60940-489-5 (hardcover : alk. paper) -- ISBN 978-1-60940-490-1 (epub ebook) -- ISBN 978-1-
60940-491-8 (kindle/mobipocket ebook) -- ISBN 978-1-60940-492-5 (library pdf)
  1. Automobiles in art. 2. Commercial art--United States--History. I. Title.
  NC825.A8H374 2015
  740'.49629222--dc23   2015012602

ACKNOWLEDGEMENTS

I first wish to acknowledge Bryce Milligan of Wings Press, who has been continually supportive
of my literary/creative efforts. Wings Press has become a first class publishing house that turns
out very high quality books. It is certainly a credit to San Antonio and Texas that it is here. I
would also like to thank Eric Edelman, who like Bryce and myself, is another outside-the-box
kind of guy. As a forward he has written an interesting introduction to engravings, line illustrations, and earlier printing methods. I am grateful to New York collage illustrator Joan Hall,
who provided me with some interesting early car images. I also want to thank Ebay dealer Steve
Antin, aka. SAAPGH, who went out of his way to supply me with some fine early car ads. For
suggestions and helpful feedback I am grateful to Terry Goodbody, Marjorie Robbins, Ed Con-
roy, and Gwyllm Llwydd. I want to acknowledge my dear relatives Kay and Carl Evans of Texas
Pneumatic Tool Co. in Reagan, Texas, who put me up during a research trip to Texas A&M.
Some of the images in this book came from the Research Center of the Panhandle-Plains His-
torical Museum in Canyon, Texas. For this I would like to thank its Director, Warren Stricker.
Finally, I am grateful to family members and friends; Bennett Kerr, Mike Harter & Monique
Dupuis, John & Marty Marmaduke, Jim & Barbara Whitton, James Hendricks, Nathan Sumar,
and Terrelita Maverick for their continued support and interest.

Contents

Contents

A Short History of the Methods of Printed Illustration,
by Eric Edelman

Introduction,
by Alan Harris

Early Automobiles:
A History in Advertising Line Art, 1890-1930

Dedication

This book is for my departed relatives, the Harters, Currys, Rickelmanns, and Shermans, who lived during the time period covered by this book, and knew many of these automobiles. As a child I got to know a number of these people; visiting them required family road trips. A part of the joy of those journeys was getting to see old relics of the past along our route, old houses and other buildings, especially of the Victorian type, steam locomotives, and rusty cars, trucks, and tractors, often in junkyards or pastures. They offered more for the imagination than anything new or contemporary. Many of the cars in this book would have populated those junkyards then, as well as more recent ones from the 1930s and 40s. They all "had their day" and then time left them behind. Like it or not, we humans also get to "have our day" and then vanish too quickly from the stage. So before this author vanishes, he wishes to leave this book as a testament to that past age as we plunge onward into the uncertain future that now awaits humanity.

A Short History of the Methods of Printed Illustration

Eric Edelman

mong his previous books, Jim Harter pictorially chronicled the history of nineteenth-century railroads—both American and foreign—through their appearance in the then-common medium of wood engraving. More recently, he published *Early Farm Tractors: A History in Advertising Line Art,* which is an older sister of *Early Automobiles.* This present work is a fascinating collection of late nineteenth- and early twentieth-century automotive illustrations taken from magazine advertising and engineering journals. It parallels Mr. Harter's railroad and tractor histories, both in its subject and how it was depicted. Almost all of the images in these two works were created as line drawings by individual artists, and printed as photoengravings.

Just as railroads began to give way to gasoline-powered internal combustion engine vehicles, wood engravings gave way to photoengravings that were faster and less labor-intensive to produce. For the first time, facsimile photographs appeared in print alongside line drawings and other artistic renditions. Wood engraving dominated the market for illustration in mass-produced books and periodicals from about 1840 until 1890. Thousands of newspapers, magazines, and books carried these engravings. Even after photoengraved illustrations had largely replaced wood engravings, the latter still appeared in some high quality books and periodicals until the 1920's.

Before the invention of wood engraving, illustrated books were expensive, and pictorial periodicals were either crude or non-existent. This was because fine illustrations had to be printed separately from the text; the engraving plates or lithographic stones used for printing the pictures were not the same height as the body of the metal type pieces from which text was printed. This meant that such illustrations would appear on separate pages bound into the book at a later production stage, or that they would be glued ("tipped-in") in gaps in text-printed pages. Older style woodcuts could print simultaneously with type, since the picture blocks could be made the same height as metal type ("type-high"), and thus could be inked and printed at the same time as type; however, the pictures were often very crude in quality because carving them against the wood grain was difficult.

Wood engraving solved the problems of high cost and low quality. Wood engravings were carved into the end grain of dense wood blocks, with almost the same tools as were used in copper engraving. Carving in the end grain of a wood block meant that an engraving tool could move equally easily in all directions, resulting in very fine lines and details in the finished print. Additionally, only the surface, uncarved portions of wood engraving blocks were inked; in effect, the wood engraver was carving the highlights of the print—the un-inked areas. When the engraving blocks were made type-high, they could be locked into the same frame as the type so that both pictures and text were inked and printed together in one pass. No longer was it necessary to print pictures separately from words. As high-quality illustrated publications increased in number, the cost of producing them decreased.

During their heyday, wood engravings found especial use in scientific and technical textbooks and magazines. The engravings were perfectly suited to rendering the fine details and intricacy of machinery. By using systems of variable size cross-hatching, lines, and dots, wood engravings achieved a broad tonal range that was ideal for portraying volumes in space. The downside to wood engraving was the length of time it took to engrave all but the simplest blocks. Extremely intricate engravings would often be created by two or more engravers working together for days, weeks, or even months.

At nearly the same time that wood engraving was thriving, two new inventions came into being that would eventually help force it into obsolescence: the rotary press and the electrotype. Yet at first, these two inventions helped spread wood engraving further than ever when combined with an earlier printing innovation: the casting of entire typeset pages to make printing plates. Casting entire pages of set type as "plates" from molds was first done in the early eighteenth century (the process was known as "stereotyping" or "cliché," which later on assumed the meanings they now have). It was a great advance in printing that extended the usefulness of hand-set movable type.

Before the invention of stereotyping, book printing was a limited, costly, and time-consuming process. Even the largest and best-furnished printing establishments had a limited amount of movable type. Once the first pages of a book were typeset by hand, they had to be printed immediately in the desired number of copies, after which the type composing them had to be taken apart to be available for resetting as future pages. Later editions of such a book would have to be completely typeset from scratch.

Stereotyping forever removed such limitations from printing. Detailed papier-mâché molds were made of every completely typeset page, and used to cast plates of such pages in type metal. It was now these plates that were used in the printing presses rather than movable type, which was then freed for other typesetting projects. Books could then be printed at any time without tying up vital handset type in new typesetting, or could be reprinted inexpensively in new editions by printing them from their stored page plates. By the middle of the nineteenth century, stereotyping dominated book publishing.

Rotary presses allowed faster printing than flat-bed models. But their printing rollers were unable to hold movable type. As a natural extension of the stereotype process, flat-set type molds were made that could be curved to cast printing plates that fitted the rotary press rollers.

Like movable type, wood engravings could not be used directly on rotary presses. Electrotyping changed that. The electrotype was a mold created by electroplating movable type or a wood engraving block with a thin layer of copper. The outside of the mold was backed and filled in with metal of a lower melting point than the copper, and curved so that the plate cast from the mold would fit on the press roller.

By the 1880's, a means of making photoengraved printing plates was perfected that would reproduce pen and ink drawings with great fidelity, but without the need to transfer them to the printing surface by hand, as with wood engraving. Zinc plates were brought into contact with photographic facsimiles of drawings printed with acid-resistant sticky ink, which transferred to the zinc plate and protected the lines that would be inked on the plate. All unprotected (un-inked and non-printing) areas of the zinc plate were etched away by a strong acid bath. In a matter of minutes, the acid could carve a plate that would have taken a human engraver days or weeks to make.

The slow pace of creating wood engravings soon made them unable to compete with quickly produced photoengravings. As a natural extension of the photoengraving method, photographs eventually appeared in books and magazines, and later in newspapers. The photographic image overtook and passed the wood-engraved image in popularity. Rotary presses and electrotyping were applied with great success to the publication of photographs.

But during the years between the decline of wood engraving illustration and the rising supremacy of photographic images in printing, line drawings done by skilled artists were photoengraved onto zinc plates for publication in books and periodicals. These printed drawings were usually simpler than the earlier engravings, but when rendered in the scratchboard technique, they had the potential for rivaling the finest wood engravings in their fineness of detail, tonal range, and portrayal of spatial volumes. They were ideal for depicting intricate machinery like that in tractors, automobiles, and other vehicles. This book is a treasury of the finest examples of that phase in the arts of printing and illustration.

Edelman Eric Edelman is a collagist and found-object sculptor. His work has been featured in one-person shows and group exhibitions in museums and private galleries, and is represented in several private and institutional collections. Edelman's collages and other work have appeared in *The New York Review of Books* and in the books *The Art of the Miniature* and *Genius in a Bottle*, as well as the monograph "Eric Edelman Collages the Unconscious."

Automobile racing began almost as soon as the horseless carriage became horseless, and quickly became popular. The early pioneers as well as the later manufacturers found it to be advantageous, as it was the best way to test an automobile for both speed and endurance. Improvements in racing vehicles impacted production models, and winning vehicles brought valuable publicity to their manufacturers, providing important name recognition.

Officially sanctioned events began as road races in Europe, but after a number of roadside spectator fatalities, closed-circuit racing became the norm. In America cars were raced on speedways in places like Indianapolis, Milwaukee, Syracuse, Tacoma, San Antonio and Waco in Texas, Elgin and Springfield in Illinois, and San Diego, Santa Monica, Los Angeles, and Sacramento in California. Among the most important of the early competitions were the Vanderbilt Cup held at Long Island, the Indianapolis 500, and the Elgin National Road Race. Mercer, Stutz, and Duesenberg were among American companies noted for their involvement in racing.

Above: 1917 Hudson "Super 6" racing model.

Below: The Duesenberg "Special" racing car (left) as it appeared in a 1925 company ad. Standard Duesenberg models were apparently never depicted in line illustration.

Introduction

Jim Harter

Many books have been published on automotive history over the past century. This has included general histories as well as biographies and memoirs of important industry figures. Other volumes have focused on certain time periods, specific auto firms, and special car categories. This present book is a pictorial history documenting the automobile from the early 1890s to 1930. It is unique for being entirely illustrated with black & white line drawings and engravings, coming from car advertisements and early engineering journals. Previous books on automobiles have almost completely overlooked this important source of imagery.

The pictures here provide an interesting outside-the-box glimpse of automotive history, expanding it and making it richer. The author made strong efforts to find as many of the images "essential" to this story as possible, but it was not always easy. For example, limiting pictorial content to line illustrations eliminated companies like Duesenberg and Cord that apparently never advertised in this manner. The author was also unable to find an engraving of a Duryea vehicle, but found images of two competing motor carriages in the historic Chicago *Times-Herald* competition of 1895.

Thus, while this research was occasionally disappointmenting, it also yielded pictures of many cars with which the viewer may be unfamiliar, including some rather beautiful ones. The overwhelming majority of these illustrations have never been published in a book before and many are quite rare, documenting long-gone brands and/or models. I hope that this book will appeal not only to automobile enthusiasts, but also to historians, engineers, artists, and designers.

In the early days of American car manufacture, many firms had only a brief existence, in some cases producing only a few vehicles. Although no complete record exists of U.S. auto companies, Wikipedia estimates that over 1,800 firms or individuals built cars in the 1896-1930 period. This figure may give some indication of the entrepreneurial spirit, innovative engineering, creative design, masses of capital, great hopes, and plain hard work that were poured into this business in its formative years.

The spirit of that time shows in the many different designs of the cars, but is also captured in the various illustration styles reproduced here. They begin late in the Victorian era when engravings were still in use and the Art Nouveau style popular, and end when Art Deco was in vogue. Many different artists produced them, using a number of different techniques, and they vary considerably in style and level of detail. While it was common practice for engravings to be signed, this was rarely the case with advertising illustrations. So the names of these artists are largely lost to us now.

The advantage of line illustration was that it produced clear bold images with strong contrasts and graphic quality. Otherwise, black & white photographs or half-tone illustrations were used, or color images, which were more expensive to print. Probably no more than five percent of car ads were of the line illustration type. This style seems to have been most popular in the years around 1912, a period when many new firms with slim advertising budgets entered the market. However, by the 1920s, line illustration was considerably less fashionable.

Automobiles, trucks, and tractors all made their historic debut about the same time. This was largely due to the development of the gasoline-powered ("gas"-powered) internal

combustion engine. It reached a point of viability in 1885 when both Gottlieb Daimler and Karl Benz built gas-powered vehicles. At this time steam carriages and traction engines had been in use for awhile, but they had serious drawbacks. However, subsequent improvements in steam technology allowed it to compete for a time with gas-power for automotive dominance. Electric vehicles were tried as well, but low battery power versus heavy battery weight proved to be an insurmountable obstacle. A substantial drawback to early gas vehicles was that they had to be hand-cranked to start. Electric starters were introduced on some luxury cars in 1912, and gas-power soon gained the upper hand.

In the beginning, Europe had a head start over the United States—and a better system of improved roads. Both Daimler and Benz continued their own efforts, and in 1891 the French firms of Panhard & Levassor and Peugeot began making cars using Daimler engines. That same year the "Systeme Panhard" was introduced; a design layout having four wheels, vertical front-mounted engine, connecting transmission, and rear-wheel drive. In the horseless carriage era most vehicles had the engine in the rear, but by the early 1900s Panhard's system had become widely adopted. America's automotive efforts reached a critical mass on Nov. 28, 1895 when a Duryea motor carriage defeated several Benz powered vehicles in Chicago's famous *Times-Herald* race.

Horseless carriages became a fad that quickly spread in the U.S., and from 1896 through 1920 many automobile manufacturers entered the marketplace, greatly increasing the nation's economic activity. Spurred by the automobile, new businesses were spawned, while others greatly expanded. This included vast expansions of road building and the petroleum industry, and the introduction of associated small businesses like gas stations, repair shops, body shops, auto parts manufacturers and dealerships, towing businesses, junk yards, roadside restaurants, roadside advertising, and roadside cabins or tourist courts where motorists might spend the night.

Demand for production materials also increased, stimulating a growth in those industries. This included steel and alloy metals, aluminum, wood, plate glass, tires, leather, and other upholstery materials. While automobiles had originally been affordable only for a wealthy elite, they soon became essential for a changing way of life. Henry Ford's Model T, first introduced in late 1908, brought a relatively cheap, well-made car to the middle class. His introduction of the moving assembly line in 1913 brought prices down, making the Model T affordable for many working class individuals. Among them were his own employees, who in 1914 had their wage almost doubled to $5 a day. Automobiles gave people more freedom and a greater sense of adventure. They reduced rural isolation, and in urban settings allowed people to live farther away from their workplaces. In time this led to a vast expansion of suburban housing.

Automobile racing quickly became popular. The early pioneers as well as the later manufacturers found it to be advantageous, as it was the best way to test an automobile for both speed and endurance. It was a competition involving both driving and engineering skill. Drivers and engineers worked together in a constant effort to improve their machines to gain an advantage over their opponents. In doing so they advanced automotive technology, raising the quality and performance level of the industry. Improvements in racing vehicles impacted production models, and winning vehicles brought valuable publicity to their manufacturers, providing important name recognition.

Officially sanctioned events began as road races in Europe, but after spectators began getting killed, closed-circuit racing became the norm. In America cars were raced on speedways in places like Indianapolis, Milwaukee, Syracuse, Tacoma, San Antonio and Waco in Texas, Elgin and Springfield in Illinois, and San Diego, Santa Monica, Los Angeles, and Sacramento in California. Among the most important of the early competitions were the Vanderbilt Cup held at Long Island for some years and then elsewhere, the Indianapolis 500, and the Elgin National Road Race. Mercer, Stutz, and Duesenberg were among American companies noted for their involvement in racing.

Besides Henry Ford, other colorful men emerged who had dreams of creating automotive empires. The earliest was Col. Albert A. Pope, who began transitioning from a bicycle empire to an automotive one in the late 1890s. Unfortunately, the financial panic of 1907 bankrupted him, eliminating three of his four companies. His last one, Pope-Hartford, went under three receiverships before collapsing in 1913. William C. Durant, who took over Buick in 1904, showed a gift for assembling giant automotive corporations, but never learned how to properly manage them. He created General Motors, lost it in 1910, took it over again in 1916, lost it again in 1920, and then in 1921 began assembling another empire: Durant Motors, which struggled into the Great Depression and then expired.

During World War I automobile companies were involved in producing staff cars, trucks, and marine and aircraft engines. At the end of the conflict, Ford controlled half the market in new car sales, and General Motors, one-fifth. Higher in status than Ford's Model T were lower-medium priced cars (up to $1,500) like Willys-Overland, Studebaker, Maxwell, Dodge Brothers, Buick, and Reo, and they became attractive for many buyers whose economic position had improved. About 1920 companies like Ford and GM became involved in financing; offering payment plans over time, and very quickly most people bought their cars that way. Firms large enough to afford mass production quickly gained an advantage over their smaller rivals. Mass production resulted in lower cost-per-unit, and companies like Ford reduced their prices to a point where smaller firms in the same price range could no longer compete. From 1923-27 the number of American car producers declined from 108 to 44.

As old companies died off, two important contenders emerged. In the early 1920s former Buick president Walter P. Chrysler took over the distressed Maxwell firm, using it as a base to launch his high-compression Chrysler in 1924. His acquisition of Dodge Brothers in 1928 provided a dealer network and production facilities sufficient to compete with GM and Ford, and he did so, immediately bringing out his Plymouth and DeSoto brands. E.L. Cord did a similar turnaround with ailing Auburn, but keeping its name, turned it into an innovative, prosperous, and respected firm. He acquired the similarly distressed Duesenberg company, and provided engineering genius Fred Duesenberg with all the money necessary to build the car of his dreams. Finally, he introduced his beautiful Cord front-wheel drive automobile, unfortunately just before the Great Depression.

	U.S. Auto Production	U.S. Auto Registration
1900	4,192	8,000
1910	181,000	458,377
1920	1,905,560	8,131,522
1925	3,735,171	
1929	5,337,087	
1930		22,972,745
1932	1,331,860	

During the 1920s, automotive technology continued to improve, and beginning about 1924, four-wheel brakes began to be offered on many cars—hydraulic for expensive brands and mechanical for cheaper ones. About this same time heaters and radios became available in a few brands as luxury options. In 1926 Ford produced its 15 millionth Model T. But in 1927 it shut down its assembly lines while it retooled to bring out the 4-cylinder Model A. This car, having improved styling and twice the horsepower of its predecessor, was necessary for competing against GM's Chevrolet. By the late 1920s, the United States was producing about 85 percent of the world's cars, of which about 10 percent were exported.

The cars of 1929 were lower and sleeker than ever before. It was the era of the classic car, with elegant brands like Packard, Mormon, Cadillac, Pierce-Arrow, Lincoln, and LaSalle depicted in colorful Art Deco-style ads. At this time closed cars (coupes, sedans, and limousines) accounted for 90 percent of new sales. This was a total reversal from 1919 when 90 percent had been open cars (roadsters, touring cars, and phaetons).

By the end of 1929, annual auto production had reached 5,337,087 units, setting a record that would last for 20 years. This was a golden moment for the industry which unfortunately couldn't last. Later that year, the Stock Market crashed and the Great Depression arrived, plunging the nation into economic chaos. By 1932 production was down to 1,331,860 cars, a reduction of 75 percent. By then, the auto industry had hunkered down and the flamboyance and extravagance of its recent past was largely gone.

The motor car brought in many changes to the world, some positive and some negative. In the latter category was a rapid increase in car-related deaths. In America there were 36 in 1900, 1,599 in 1910, 12,155 in 1920, and 31,204 in 1930. Yet, as car technology and road systems improved, there was a significant reduction of overall deaths in relation to the total mileage driven.

Cars and buses changed people's traveling habits and strongly impacted the railroad industry. Although providing improvement in many cases, this ultimately led to the destruction of much of America's world-class passenger train network, and the virtual elimination of electric interurban and streetcar systems. In the latter case, between 1936 and 1950, General Motors and its allies in the tire and petroleum businesses funded National City Lines and Pacific City Lines. These firms systematically bought up over 100 trolley and interurban lines in 45 cities, ripped out the track, and replaced them with bus systems. The goal wasn't only to sell buses, tires, and fuel, but to wean people off of public transportation in order to sell more cars.

Of significant importance was the way the American landscape was changed to accommodate the automobile. The U.S. quickly became the most auto-centric country on the planet, building immense highway systems. Vast developments of tract housing resulted in blighted landscapes, urban sprawl, ugly architecture, strip malls, traffic congested roads, and commutes lasting for hours. The "flight to the suburbs" and resultant inner-city decay all owe much to the automobile, with Detroit, the "Motor City," ironically becoming the prime example of what could go wrong.

Using the hindsight of the present, we can glimpse some of the environmental damage that has been done: asphalt surface runoff, illegal dumping, and oil spills have been important factors in the pollution of rivers, oceans, and likely, aquifers. Auto emissions have contributed to respiratory ailments, other health afflictions, and acid rain, but more importantly to the accumulation of greenhouse gases, which today threaten us with the ominous spectre of global warming. Switzerland's great psychologist Carl G. Jung once observed that for every good that comes into the world, there also comes a corresponding evil, and this certainly seems true for the motor car. Thus, while it is important to recognize this Faustian dimension, this book celebrates the automobile in an earlier, more innocent time, when it seemed to open up bright sunny vistas for humanity's future.

Among the pictures in this book are early models of still-existing brands like Ford, Cadillac, Buick, Chevrolet, and Chrysler. Then there are examples of cars popular or prestigious in their day, like Packard, Studebaker, Pierce-Arrow, Stutz, Jordan, Franklin, Maxwell, Overland, and Auburn. Finally, there are many more images of largely forgotten brands like Starr, Velie, King, Queen, HAL, K-R-I-T, Stephens, Palmer-Singer, and Diana. The few examples of foreign automobiles here include Rolls-Royce, Napier, Renault, and Fiat. Well represented are various body styles: buggies, runabouts, roadsters, touring cars, coupes, coaches, sedans, landaulets, limousines, broughams, and town cars; ranging from the slow, quaint, and primitive to the speedy, elegant, and showy.

Many images here came from popular publications like *Colliers, Country Life, House & Garden, Life, Literary Digest, National Geographic,* and *Saturday Evening Post.* Others came from automotive trade publications like *The Automobile Trade Journal, The Automobile, Horseless Age, Motor,* and *Motor Age.* Agricultural journals like *Country Gentleman, Farm & Ranch, Farm Life, Implement & Vehicle Journal,* and *Progressive Farmer* contributed others. Late 19th century science and engineering journals like *The Engineer* and *La Nature: Revue des Sciences* provided the really early engravings. All of these pictures have been organized chronologically, in so far as possible.

In preparing this book I have included the best line-style images I was able to find. These have been scanned either at 1,200 or 2,400 dpi. Some were removed from a larger pictorial context, and all have been touched up to improve graphic quality. Although this book is primarily pictorial, its text and captions have been written with the intention of providing a solid framework for understanding this history. This work has been a labor of love for its author, and he wishes you the reader, a most enjoyable and interesting experience.

Early Automobiles

A History in Advertising Line Art, 1890-1930

This image is from the Nov. 12, 1887 issue of the French journal, *La Nature: Revue des Sciences*. It shows an early ancestor of today's automobiles, a three-wheel steam carriage built by M.J. Virot, head engineer at l'Ecole Centrale Lyonnaise, Lyon, France. The purpose of the man blowing the horn was to alert any traffic that was ahead.

STEAM CARRIAGE ANCESTORS

Today's automobiles are the result of a long process of technological evolution. This evolution didn't begin with the motorcar, but extends back to earlier innovations in carriage, wagon, and bicycle design. This accumulated knowledge provided essential technological knowhow for automotive development in its formative years. Equally essential for the automobile was having a reliable power source. Contending for this role in the early years were the steam engine, the gas-powered internal combustion engine, and battery-powered electrical motors. All of these technologies went through their own developmental phases, all had positive and negative qualities, and it took a while before a clear winner was decided.

Of these, the steam engine came first, and the story of its use for powering road vehicles is an interesting one. In the 1760s Englishman James Watt developed a workable steam engine from one developed earlier by Thomas Newcomen. In this process, coal or wood was burned, heating water to the boiling point where it produced steam. This steam was then carried to a cylinder where its pressure would drive a piston rotating on an axle. This converted reciprocating motion into rotary motion. While steam engines were first adapted for industrial manufacturing purposes, it wasn't long before they they were tried out as a power source for transportation.

The first steam-powered road vehicle was built in 1769 by the Frenchman Nicholas Cugnot. Intended as a tricycle-type, self-propelled gun carriage, it was powered by two single-acting vertical engines operating alternately on a driving axle. Sometime later, experiments in England resulted in steam carriages built by William Murdock in 1784, William Symington in 1786, and Robert Fourness of Halifax in 1788. Symington's vehicle was powered by a low-pressure Watt condensing engine, and had a rack-and-ratchet drive. While none of these efforts were really successful, they furthered experimentation in this field, helping to pave the way for more successful machines later.

Steam engines at this time were very heavy in relation to the power they produced. If they were to have any practicality for powering vehicles, it was necessary to improve the weight/power ratio. Raising steam pressure would do this, but it increased the risk of boiler explosion. In the late 1790s Richard Trevithick of Cornwall began experiments with higher-pressure steam. On Christmas eve, 1801, he successfully tested a steam carriage that carried 7 to 8 passengers. His next important creation, the world's first steam locomotive, was built in Shropshire in 1803. It began the history of railroads, and gained him lasting fame. Oliver Evans of Philadelphia developed a high-pressure steam engine that he adapted for industrial use in 1802. This was followed two years later by his strange creation, the "Oructor Amphibolis" a steam-powered scow on wheels. It was capable of moving on both land and water.

However, Aside from Evans' work and earlier experiments by Nathan Read of Salem, Massachusetts, there was relatively little interest at this time for such vehicles in America. Compared to Britain, its road system was very crude. Much transportation then was by water, but the introduction of railroads about 1830 allowed the country a way of vastly improving its transportation system. Rail travel had the advantage of being faster and cheaper than road travel. National attention became focused on railroad development, and by the 1850s lines reached the Mississippi River, and by 1869, California. Improved roads of the kind in Britain were only possible where a sufficient population and level of wealth existed to support them. Aside from a few east coast cities, America's population in the early 1800s was sparse. It was poorer and in a more primitive state. So there was relatively little interest in road development and self-propelled vehicles for decades to come.

English roads owed something to the Romans, who had constructed some very good ones during their occupation of the country, and which to some degree remained in existence many centuries later. In the early 19th century the Scotsmen Thomas Telford and John McAdam separately developed schemes to improve roads by laying down layers of specific kinds of rocks. For this Telford owed some of his inspiration to the Frenchman Pierre-Marie-Jerome Tresaguet who had made similar improvements in France during the latter part of the 18th century.

The existence of these improved roads was an incentive for building steam vehicles to carry passengers commercially. A rather elaborate steam coach was built by W.H. James and Sir James Anderson in 1810. It was powered by two engines, each separately driving a rear wheel. In 1824 Walter Hancock built the first of ten steam passenger carriages. by 1836 he had finished nine and was operating them in London. In a twenty-week period, five of these traveled 4,200 miles between Stratford, Paddington, and Islington, and carried a total of 12,761 passengers.

Hancock's vehicles had some interesting names, among them "Infant," "Era," "Automaton," and "Autopsy." About 1827 James Nasmyth built a successful steam carriage capable of carrying 6 to 8 passengers. It ran for some months on the Queensferry Road near Edinburgh before being dismantled. About this same time Goldsworth Gurney built a 21-passenger coach, the first of a number, and soon began carrying passengers between Gloucester and Cheltenham.

Col. Francis Maceroni and John Squire, two of Gurney's former associates, designed a multi-tubular boiler whose working pressure was around 150 psi. The resultant boilers were incorporated into a number of steam carriages they built. These operated at speeds up to ten miles per hour. On July 18, 1833 one of them began a shuttle service between Paddington and Edgeware in London. A more ambitious undertaking was the highly ornamented steam coach built by Dr. Church in 1832. Having 22 inside and 22 outside seats, it operated at speeds up to 14 miles per hour, and ran for a time between London and Birmingham.

Among the best designed of these early machines were some built by John Scott Russell of Edinburgh. They apparently could climb steep hills and operate at speeds up to 17 mph. A number were put in operation in 1834 by the Steam Carriage Co. of Scotland, running between Glasgow and Paisley. While having a seating capacity of 26, they often carried 30 to 40 passengers, some riding on a tender pulled in the rear. Three persons were involved in the operation of these machines: the steersman sat in the front seat, the engine-driver sat in the rear above the engines, with gauges close by, and the stoker stood below on the footplate near the boiler.

However, for various reasons, public objections were raised. After a fatal boiler explosion occurred in Paisley on July 29, 1834, Russell's vehicles were withdrawn from service and subsequently outlawed in Scotland. Steam carriages were disliked for a number of reasons. Their coal smoke produced irritating and noxious fumes. They were noisy and gave off steam exhaust. Often they frightened horses, and presented the danger of a boiler explosion. When operated at higher speeds they frightened some, not only riding passengers, but other traffic on the road. Finally, those in the omnibus and stage coach businesses feared their competition, as did the newly emerging railways.

J.W. Boulton of Ashton-under-Lyne built a number of steam carriages beginning in 1848. These were mainly of the small "pleasure" variety, likely intended for estate use. In the 1850s both Thomas Rickett and H. Percy Holt built a few similar carriages, all of 3-wheel design. Of somewhat greater passenger capacity was a 4-wheeled carriage built by Yarrow & Hilditch in 1862. A skillfully designed 3-wheeled "Steam Wagonette" was developed by Catley & Ayres from 1863-7.

Meanwhile, the railway and stagecoach companies had begun working together against their competition. Beginning in 1836 legislation was enacted subjecting self-propelled, non-rail vehicles to excessive fees and tolls, which significantly hurt their operations. Later, in 1865, the Locomotives Act was passed. This limited self-propelled vehicles to a speed of four mph on public roads, and required a man with a red flag to precede them. Only repealed in 1896, this law greatly discouraged further improvements of this technology in Britain. But inventive efforts still went on in improving steam traction engines for farm use and road locomotives for goods haulage.

Elsewhere, however, interest in passenger vehicles increased. Inventors in countries like France, Germany, and the US began to experiment, not only with steam carriages, but later with gas and electrical power. Things began slowly in America. In the 1850s New Yorker Richard Dudgeon built a 10-passenger steam vehicle. Performing well, it was exhibited at New York's Crystal Palace. Unfortunately, this building was destroyed by fire in 1858 and Dudgeon's carriage was lost. After the Civil War he built another steam vehicle, but at the time there seemed to be little interest in it. The Nov. 28, 1863 issue of *Scientific American* reported on a 2-passenger steam carriage built by Sylvester H. Roper of Roxbury, Massachusetts. Essentially a buggy with a vertical boiler engine at the rear, it developed 2-hp and reached speeds of 20 mph. Afterwards it became an attraction at fairs and circus sideshows.

EARLY DEVELOPMENTS IN GAS PROPULSION AND MOTOR CARRIAGES

Pioneering efforts with the internal combustion engine begin with John Barber who built a crude motor fueled by coal gas in 1790. Robert Street built a turpentine-powered engine in 1794. In 1860 the Belgian Jean Joseph Etienne Lenoir filed a French patent for a 1-cylinder 2-stroke (2-cycle) engine designed to use vaporous illuminating gas. In 1862 Alphonse Beau de Roches filed a French patent describing the principle of the 4-stroke (4-cycle) engine. By 1863 Lenoir was operating a small vehicle powered by an engine producing 1.5-hp at 100 rpm. However, it was heavy and inefficient, and the 2-stroke design was not yet successful. Siegfried Marcus of Vienna was later authorized to build motor carriages using Lenoir's engine. Apparently these were not very successful, but his second vehicle, built in 1875, still exists today in Vienna's Technisches Museum.

During the 1860s, the Germans Nikolaus August Otto and Eugen Langen formed a company to build an improved version of Lenoir's motor. After winning a gold medal at the 1867 Paris World Exhibition, they continued their efforts, and in 1876 introduced the much quieter 4-stroke Otto gas engine. In his book *The Illustrated History of Tractors,* Robert Moorhouse notes that this new motor introduced the "basic engine cycle of operation used today... 1. Induction of the air and fuel mixture, 2. Compression of the mixture, 3. Power from the burning of the fuel, 4. Exhaustion of the burnt gases and so back to induction."

Otto and Langen's firm became known as Gasmotoren Fabrik Deutz AG in 1880. Working for the company at this time were Wilhelm Mayback and Gottlieb Daimler. This pair subsequently left the firm and began engine experiments using a liquid petroleum derivative called benzin (gasoline) for fuel. They developed a 900 rpm engine in 1885 and used it to power a motorized bicycle. About this same time Karl Benz, a German builder of gas motors, built a 4-stroke engine and adapted it to power a tricycle. It is interesting to note that despite the later association of their names, Daimler and Benz never met.

Gasoline was one of the products that resulted from crude oil processing. During the 19th century it was done in a number of European countries. In America, Edwin L. Drake was the first to produce it commercially at Titusville, Pennsylvania, in 1859. Other products included kerosene, fuel oil, lubricant oils, waxes, and asphalt. Kerosene quickly replaced whale oil for lamp fuel, and the other products found uses also, but it took longer for volatile gasoline to find its special niche, as fuel for the internal combustion engine. Its advantages were that it vaporized quickly, was rich in heat energy, and that the crude oil from which it came apparently existed in vast quantities underground.

Otto's 1876 engine produced 3-hp at 180 rpm. By 1885, however, Daimler's engines ran about 800 rpm. and he had reduced the ratio of weight per unit of horsepower from about 1,000 lbs. to less than 100. In 1889 Daimler patented two different 2-cylinder engines, a V-2 with cylinders inclined 15 degrees, and one where the cylinders were horizontally opposed. In 1891 the French firms of Panhard & Levassor and Peugeot began production of motor carriages using Daimler engines. The second Panhard carriage built was the first to have a front-mounted engine. It set a precedent for a layout that became widely copied in the industry: a vertical front-mounted engine, connecting transmission, and rear-wheel drive. It was called *la Systeme Panhard.* The firm began designing its own engines in 1895.

While Daimler had invented a hot tube ignition system, Benz devised one having an electric spark. His 1885 tricycle, powered by a single cylinder engine, ran at speeds of 6-10 mph. Moving to 4-wheel designs, Benz continued his work and built a factory in Mannheim. By 1894 his company was producing 500 motor vehicles per year.

In the 1876 Centennial Exposition in Philadelphia, a 3-cylinder 2-stroke engine was exhibited. Built by George Brayton of Providence, Rhode Island, its intended use was for powering a streetcar. A Rochester patent lawyer, George B. Selden, saw the engine and began to think of its possibilities for powering carriages. In May 1879 he applied for a patent for a "road engine" using a liquid hydrocarbon fuel, a steering mechanism, and a device that could disengage the engine from the driving wheels. It is unclear whether Selden actually intended to build this vehicle. Instead, he may have hoped that sometime in the future he could collect royalties for patenting this idea before anyone else. He didn't seek approval right away, but instead filed successive amendments, keeping the application pending until a more auspicious moment arrived—in this case, until Nov. 5, 1895. This would soon become a problem for this newly emerging industry.

In the 1870s-90s bicycles became popular in Western countries. In the beginning high-wheeled velocipedes were used, but they required considerable physical strength, and largely limited this sport to hardy men (trousers were also required). In 1877, cyclist J.K. Starley of Coventry, England, devised the first differential, and in 1885 he introduced his "safety" bicycle. Having low-wheels, chain-drive, and gearing, it made bicycle riding much easier and accessible for women and children. Bicycling rapidly became very popular in America, and one result was that it raised awareness about the poor quality of roads.

The Good Roads Movement was officially launched in May 1880 in Newport, Rhode Island. In January 1892, the League of American Wheelmen, an organization of bicyclists, began publication of *Good Roads Magazine*. This group successfully petitioned state and local authorities for road improvements. Congress appropriated $10,000 in 1893 for a Department of Agriculture study on improved methods of highway construction. The Office of Road Inquiry was established that year as a branch within the Department. This began a process that ultimately led to the formation of the Bureau of Public Roads and to federal highway assistance, but these improvements were over two decades away. In 1900, outside of major cities, there were only about 200 miles of hard-surfaced roadways.

In his book *The American Automobile: A Brief History*, John B. Rae notes a number of contributions the bicycle made to motor car development: "There were other influences besides the stimulation of highway travel. From the bicycle manufacturers the early automobile industry inherited steel-tube framing that combined strength with lightness, the chain drive, ball and roller bearings, and differential gearing. The vital role of the bicycle in preparing the way for the automobile is strikingly illustrated in the long roster of men and companies who moved from one industry to the other; prominent on the list are Morris in England, Opel in Germany, and Duryea, Pope, Winton, and Willys in the United States."

EARLY DEVELOPMENT OF ELECTRIC VEHICLES

Thomas Davenport, a Brandon, Vermont blacksmith, was fascinated by magnets. He constructed in 1834 what was perhaps the world's first electric motor. He then devised a second motor that propelled itself around a small track in the manner of a toy train. In 1839 the Scotsman Robert Davidson created a 6-ton electric locomotive. For power a primitive galvanic battery was devised. When power was needed some 78 pairs of zinc and iron plates were lowered into a container of sulphuric acid. To cut off the power, these plates were raised out again. In 1850 Professor Charles G. Page devised a ring-shaped iron bar, apparently the world's first armature.

Zenobie Theophile Gramme, a Belgian, invented the first successful dynamo generator in 1870. Essentially an iron cylinder enclosed in a coil of copper wire, it could be driven by the motion of waterpower or a steam engine to generate electrical power. Two years later Gramme discovered that his dynamo could also function as a motor, receiving electric current and converting it into motion. In 1880 France's Gaston Plante invented the first rechargeable storage battery, a great improvement over the galvanic type. Soon storage batteries were tested out for railway and tramway use. After America's Frank Sprague made improvements in electric motor design in 1884, this technology showed potential for road vehicle use.

America's first battery-powered carriage to successfully operate was built by William Morrison of Des Moines, Iowa, between 1888 and 1890. A 3-seat sulky, it could carry six passengers, and had hand-bar steering. Powered by a 4-hp streetcar motor, it carried 24 storage battery cells beneath the seat. Single-reduction gearing was used for transferring motive power to the rear axle. On a smooth level road this vehicle could maintain a speed of ten mph. Harold Sturges of Chicago's American Battery Company later bought it and used it for demonstration purposes at the 1893 Columbian Exposition.

In 1892 the Holtzer-Cabot Electric Co. of Brookline, Massachusetts, built an 8-passenger brake style carriage for wealthy Bostonian Fiske Warren. The firm built a similar vehicle in 1895 that carried up to seven. Producing 7.5-hp, its motor weighed 450 lbs. The splendid coachwork and upholstery were done by Chauncey Thomas & Co., of Boston.

In 1894, Henry G. Morris and Pedro Salom of Philadelphia built their first "Electrobat" carriage, and the following year it went into commercial production. Both an Electrobat and Sturges' (built by William Morrison) electric vehicle were entered in America's first official horseless carriage race, Chicago's *Times-Herald* competition of Nov. 28, 1895. Unfortunately, icy road conditions prevented either from finishing the race, and a gas-powered Duryea was the winner. The Electrobat used in the event was a two-passenger runabout. It had 40" diameter wheels in front, and 28" in the rear. Powered by two 1.5-hp Lundell motors, its driving gears were attached to the front axle. In good conditions on a smooth road it could reach speeds of 20 mph.

The first horseless carriage race on an American track took place at Narragansett Park during the Rhode Island State Fair of September 7, 1896. Although five Duryea vehicles were entered, the winner was a Riker Electric Stanhope; placing second was an Electrobat. Production of the Electrobat ceased in 1897, but the partners' Electric Carriage & Wagon Co. began producing electric hansom cabs for New York and Philadelphia. In the fall of 1897 this firm was taken over by Isaac L. Rice's Electric Vehicle Co.

AMERICA'S FIRST SUCCESSFUL MOTOR CARRIAGE

Reading a *Scientific American* report on Benz's vehicle in 1889 were two brothers, Charles E. and J. Frank Duryea of Springfield, Massachusetts. The brothers, who were bicycle mechanics, became determined to build their own motorized carriage. Charles, eight years older than his sibling, did most of the work in planning it and later he employed Frank to build it. Considerable research was done, including learning about the Otto engine, studying Benz's patents, talking with others in their field interested in this technology, and making engineering drawings.

While most flywheels at this time were vertical and crankshafts horizontal, Benz's flywheels were horizontal and his crankshafts vertical. Charles Duryea borrowed this idea but placed the flywheel forward of the engine rather than in the rear. This eliminated the need for a longer drive belt. Tiller steering and hot tube ignition were used, the flywheel was turned by hand for starting, and there was no muffler. Once completed, their 1-cylinder engine operated at about 500 rpm and produced 2-hp. For the carriage body, Charles purchased a used ladies' phaeton. Soon, however, business necessity required him to move to Peoria, Illinois. Leaving in September 1892, he didn't return for over two years. Thus it was left to brother Frank to complete and test the vehicle. It was first driven in Springfield on September 21, 1893.

Following this Frank built a 2-cylinder, 4-hp carriage and entered it in Chicago's Novermber 28, 1895 *Times-Herald* competition. Competing against him were the aforementioned electric vehicles, and three Benz powered carriages. The course was over 55 miles of icy streets and roads from Jackson Park to Evanston and back. The Duryea vehicle won with an average speed of 5 mph, and the only other carriage to finish was Oscar Mueller's Benz. Mueller had passed out from exposure and so the race umpire, engineer Charles Brady King, took over and finished the race while holding on to Mueller with one arm.

The Duryea Motor Wagon Co. was formed by the brothers in Springfield in 1895, producing 13 belt-drive vehicles in 1896. In 1898 the firm was moved to Peoria. Because of disputes, however, their company soon dissolved. Subsequently, Charles built cars in places like Reading, Pennsylvania; Waterloo, Iowa; and Saginaw, Michigan. In 1901 Frank made an arrangement with the J. Stevens Arms and Tool Co. of Chicopee Falls, Massachusetts. This resulted in the Stevens-Duryea Co., which manufactured fashionable automobiles until it ran out of operating capital in 1915. At this time Frank retired. After World War I the company was reformed and built cars for a time, but Duryea was no longer involved. The brothers' machine of 1893 is generally considered America's first successful automobile. But disregarding electric and steam vehicles there were three other claimants for this distinction.

In 1891 John W. Lambert built a 3-wheel vehicle in Ohio City, Ohio. Operating successfully, it used gasoline for fuel, and had electric ignition and a carburetor. However, Lambert was unsuccessful in trying to sell it and soon gave up the project. Shortly afterwards he organized the Buckeye Manufacturing Co. in Anderson, Indiana to build stationary gasoline engines. In 1902 he built the short-lived Union car, and from 1906-17 the Lambert automobile.

Henry Nadig of Allentown, Pennsylvania built a 4-wheel, 2-passenger horseless carriage in 1891. His 1-cylinder 2-hp engine had two flywheels and operated at 600-800 rpm. Mounted on a wagon chassis, it featured wooden wheels with metal rims and belt drive. Nadig filed no patents and apparently had no intent to manufacture motor carriages, as his primary business was building gasoline engines. Later, he and his sons built two more vehicles.

The other claimant was Elwood Haynes, of Kokomo, Indiana. A former teacher, he had gotten involved in the natural gas business. While making frequent inspection trips in a horse and buggy, he began to think about creating a motorized vehicle. In 1893 he enlisted the aid of two local machinist, Elmer and Edgar Apperson. In addition to providing them with sketches of his idea, he supplied a 1-cylinder, 2-stroke Sintz engine. They agreed to help him and went to work. However, this machine wasn't finished until 1894, thus invalidating Haynes' claim of being the nation's first. A motorized buggy with 28-inch bicycle wheels and tiller steering, it had three forward gears, but no reverse. Its first public test run was made on July 4 of that year on Kokomo's Pumpkinvine Turnpike, at an average speed of 6 mph. While Haynes and the Appersons began building the Haynes-Apperson vehicle in 1898, they had an acrimonious split in 1901. Afterwards they had nothing to do with each other and separately built cars in Kokomo; Haynes to 1925 and the Appersons to 1926.

STEAM REVISITED

The steam carriages of the 1890s bore little resemblance to their earlier ancestors. Most of them were smaller and designed for personal use. Coal was rarely used for fuel any longer and the engines were smaller, lighter, and of more compact design. Instead, kerosene or gasoline heated the boiler. As before, all boilers were of the fire-tube type. This meant that hot gases from the fire ran through many different tubes passing through the water contained in the boiler. This raised water temperature to the boiling point, producing the steam to power the engine. While engine and boiler designs varied, one big problem remained: boilers had to be preheated 20 minutes or more before sufficient steam built up for operation.

In 1888, the French engineer Leon Serpollet received a patent for a "steam generator." As he continued improving this technology, his "flash boiler" or "instantaneous generator," ultimately reduced preheating time to 2-3 minutes. It also allowed superheated steam to be built up to pressure levels of 600 psi. Serpollet's solution was to reverse the system from fire-tube to water-tube. In the boiler were a number of thick flattened coiled steel tubes through which water passed. When the engine was operating, at each stroke a pump injected water into the tubes to generate steam. This was heated at a high enough temperature where it was instantly converted into high pressure steam, with no danger of bursting. As the amount of steam was proportional to the amount of water, regulating water supply was critical for controlling both engine power and vehicle speed.

For heating, vaporized kerosene was fed into a burner. The lever controlling water supply also controlled the flow of burner fuel, thus insuring a synchronous operation. Gardner-Serpollet motor carriages, first introduced in 1896, employed this technology, and also had a condenser where engine steam was exhausted. This both reduced noise and recaptured part of the water, which when recycled, allowed the vehicle to travel a greater distance. The first use of this technology in America was in the 1900 White Steamer.

On Nov. 14, 1896, the Locomotives Act was repealed in Britain. This eliminated restrictive speed limits and red flag requirements for self-propelled vehicles. To celebrate "Emancipation Day" a motor carriage run from London to Brighton was held. Afterwards a number of British firms began building steam carriages. This group included Clarkson,

Ltd., builder of the Chelmsford; Albany Manufacturing Co., maker of the Lamplough-Albany; Speedwell Motor & Engineering Co., builder of the Gardner-Serpollet; The Motor Construction Co., Nottingham; and Miesse Steam Motor Syndicate, Wolverhampton. American steam vehicle builders included International Motor Car Co., maker of the Toledo, Toledo, Ohio (1901-03); The Locomobile Co. of America, Bridgeport, Connecticut (1899-1904); Prescott Automobile Manufacturing Co., Passaic, New Jersey (1901-5); the Weston Co., Passaic, New Jersey (1901); White Sewing Machine Co., Cleveland, Ohio (1900-11); and Whitney Motor Wagon Co., Boston, Massachusetts (1896-1900). In all, over 100 American firms would build steam vehicles.

The most famous of these was the Stanley steamer. In 1896, the identical Stanley twins, Francis E. and Freelan O., saw a steam carriage built by George Whitney at a fair in Brockton, Massachusetts. This inspired them to build a better one of their own. They finished it in 1897, using a 2-cylinder vertical engine and fire-tube boiler. By the time the Stanleys entered a Boston speed and hill-climbing competition in 1898, they had built two more. Their vehicle placed well in two events, then impressively won the most difficult, an 80-foot incline contest. Subsequently receiving over 200 inquiries from would-be buyers, they decided to go into business, establishing themselves in Watertown, Massachusetts.

Early in this venture, however, they were approached by John Brisben Walker, publisher of *Cosmopolitan* magazine. Walker was interested in going into the automobile business, and after agreeing to an exorbitant price, purchased the Stanley operation. This became the origin of The Locomobile Company of America which built this steamer, first in Watertown, and later in Bridgeport, Connecticut, until 1904. Afterwards Locomobile built only gas-powered cars, and these of very high quality.

The Stanleys designed a new vehicle in 1901 and reentered the business at a new factory in Newton, Massachusetts. In 1902 this became the Stanley Motor Carriage Co. By 1906 the tiller had been replaced by a steering wheel and the boiler was relocated to the front under a hood. That year in Daytona, Florida, the streamlined Stanley "Rocket" racer, driven by Fred Marriott, established a remarkable speed record of 127.66 mph. For this achievement, Stanley received England's 1906 Dewar Trophy, an award for the car whose technical innovations or performance best advanced the automotive industry. During this time the firm's main steam competitor was the more expensively built White. However, in 1911 White shifted all production over to gasoline vehicles.

In 1912, Cadillac and a few other companies introduced the electric self-starter. This eliminated the main advantage that steam cars had over their gas-powered rivals. Afterwards the Stanley firm went into a slow decline. The Steam Vehicle Corporation of America took over production in 1924, introducing cheaper models, but this only lasted to 1927.

Automotive history has largely overlooked the Doble steamer, the finest steam car ever built. Its maker, Abner Doble, born in San Francisco in 1895, built a steam vehicle while in high school and later attended Massachusetts Institute of Technology. After approaching the Stanley brothers with some of his ideas and receiving rejection, he decided to build his own cars. His 2-cylinder Model A, built in 1912, had a water-tube boiler and a special radiator that condensed all exhaust steam. Only five of these vehicles were built.

Doble made further improvements on this technology before he was joined by C.L.

Lewis to form General Engineering Co. in Detroit. The company announced production for 1917 models and received considerable attention, much of it from interested dealers and investors. Over 11,000 orders for Doble cars were placed, but because of wartime needs the US government suddenly cut off all steel to the company. Thus only a few Model C cars were built.

After a subsequent failed venture in 1919, Doble returned to San Francisco, joining with two of his brothers to form Doble Steam Motors of California in 1920. Production of the 2-cylinder Model D was followed in 1923 by Doble's 4-cylinder Model E. These cars, which featured a monotube steam generator, were silent, fast, and had beautifully styled bodies by Murphy. Capable of going over 90 mph and selling from $8,800 to $11,200, they were prized by the rich and famous. Both the actress Norma Talmadge and industrialist Howard Hughes owned one. Unfortunately, beginning in 1924, the company had legal problems resulting from manipulations by stock dealers and speculators. Doble was liquidated in 1931, following the onset of the Great Depression.

FIN DE SIECLE

In November 1895, E.P. Ingersoll founded *The Horseless Age,* the first trade publication devoted to the motor carriage. Its first issue mentioned 73 different firms that were involved with this technology. In 1896 the French word "automobile" entered the American vocabulary, and it seemed to bring with it a new spirit of automotive activity. Soon after finishing Oscar Mueller's race in the *Chicago Times-Herald* competition, Charles Brady King returned to Detroit to finish up a motor carriage he had been working on. He mounted a 4-cylinder, water-cooled engine of his own creation onto a wooden-wheeled open cart. The *Detroit Journal* of March 7, 1896, reported that King drove his vehicle down St. Antoine Street, turning onto Jefferson Avenue, then onto Woodward Avenue, arriving at the Russell House Hotel on Cadillac Square a little after 11 p.m. King's vehicle was thus the first horseless carriage to be driven in Detroit, providing an inauguration of sorts for her future role as the "Motor City." Ironically, Henry Ford is said to have followed King's excursion on a bicycle.

On June 4 of that year, Ford, an engineer at Detroit's Edison Illuminating Co., first tried out his own 2-cylinder, 4-hp "Quadricycle." It had tiller steering and bicycle style wheels, but no brakes or reverse gear. King, a friend of Ford, became the first passenger to ride in the vehicle. In the summer of 1896, Ransom Eli Olds drove a 1-cylinder, 5-hp motor carriage in Lansing, Michigan. Olds had a longtime interest in self-propulsion, having previously built a couple of steam carriages. His Olds Motor Vehicle Co. was established on Aug. 21, 1897, first producing 1-cylinder vehicles with tiller steering and a 2-speed planetary transmission.

A couple of important races were run in 1896. On Memorial Day, Frank Duryea won a race from New York to Irvington and back, receiving *Cosmopolitan* magazine's award of $3,000. In September, as previously mentioned, a Riker Electric Stanhope triumphed over five Duryea vehicles at Rhode Island's Narragansett Park. That same month Alexander

Winton's first motor carriage was completed at his Cleveland bicycle works. On May 30, 1897, a Winton vehicle reached a speed of 33.3 mph. On July 28 of that year, a Winton began a trip from Cleveland to New York, where it arrived ten days later.

Another important auto pioneer was Hiram Maxim. He had begun work on a vehicle in 1893, and in late 1894 gave it a test run down a hill, unfortunately running it into a ravine. In 1895 Maxim visited Pope Manufacturing Co., one of America's largest bicycle making firms, in Hartford, Connecticut. His initial proposal of making a motorized tricycle was rejected, but he was hired to start a motor carriage division within the company. His boss, Col. Albert A. Pope, preferred electrics over gas-powered vehicles, but Maxim's interest was in the latter. Thus both technologies were tried; the first vehicle produced being the Columbia Electric in 1897.

Maxim's early experiments with gas vehicles were less than successful, but his Columbia Mark VIII of 1899 was considered the most advanced American car of its time. Designed in the Panhard style, it had the radiator in front and a 1-cylinder engine mounted vertically behind. Other features included automatic spark advance, sliding gear transmission, shaft drive to beveled gears, and rather than a tiller, a steering wheel mounted on the left side. That year Maxim drove this vehicle in a 5-mile race against a Stanley Steamer at Branford, Connecticut. The Stanley gained the early advantage but as its steam pressure waned the Columbia passed it, winning by 1/8th of a mile. Columbia was sold by Pope in 1899, but just after the turn of the century he started a new motor carriage venture.

At this time, a horseless carriage craze was beginning that would soon sweep the country. One early event was held on Sep. 7, 1899, in Newport, Rhode Island, a summer enclave of the wealthy social elite. An obstacle course was set up on the grounds of the O.H.P. Belmont estate to test the driving skills of the participants. Preceding the event was a parade of motor vehicles down the city's fashionable Bellevue Avenue. Leading the parade was Mr. Belmont and Mrs. Stuyvesant Fish in a runabout covered with yellow flowers. Coming next was Mrs. Belmont with James W. Gerard, a future US ambassador to Germany. Participating in the competition were such notables as Harry Lehr, Col. Jack Astor, and Reginald Ronalds; the latter two recent veterans of the Spanish-American conflict in Cuba.

VIVA LE FRANCE

In 1894, the publication *Le Petit Journal* organized a Paris to Rouen run of about 78 miles to test which vehicles were most economical and reliable. Of the over 100 motor carriages entered, 14 were gas-powered and all the rest steam. The fastest was a De Dion Bouton steam carriage which averaged 12 mph, but it was penalized because it required a crew of two. A Peugeot and Panhard performed best among the gasoline entries and split the first prize.

The following year, a 732-mile race was held from Paris to Bordeaux and back. However the event actually began at Versailles. Fifteen gas carriages, six steamers, and one electric began the race, with eight gas and one steam vehicle finishing. Arriving at Paris'

Porte Maillot 48 hours and 48 minutes later was Emile Levassor, a partner in the Panhard & Lavassor firm. Preferring not to relinquish his Panhard to a relief driver midway, he had covered the entire distance himself, averaging 14.91 mph. Powering his carriage was a 2-cylinder, 4-hp modified Daimler engine. Among the entrants of this race were two Americans, William K. Vanderbilt Jr. and James Gordon Bennett. Bennett, publisher of the *New York Herald*, subsequently sponsored the international Gordon Bennett Cup races from 1900-05. Vanderbilt went on to sponsor the Vanderbilt Cup Races held in Long Island from 1904-10, and then elsewhere through 1916.

Louis Renault had been a bit of a black sheep in his Parisian bourgeois family. But he had a mechanical gift for creating inexpensive, light automobiles that ran very well. In 1898 he won a competition racing a 550-pound runabout up Montmartre's steep Rue Lepic, and soon patented his direct drive system. His two brothers, Marcel and Fernand, decided to join him in setting up Renault Freres in 1899, establishing their works on the Isle de Seguin in Paris. In the Paris-Toulouse-Paris race of 1900 the only cars to finish in the light-car class were three Renaults.

In 1902, a race was held from Paris to Vienna, a distance of 615 miles. Winning the event in 15 hours and 46 minutes was Marcel Renault, driving a lightweight Renault. A 70-hp Panhard won the heavy-car class with a time of 16 hours and 26 minutes. The most difficult part of the trip was through the steep Arlberg Pass, and on the dangerous descent the brakes of some cars caught fire, with drivers having to leap from their vehicles in order to save themselves.

Clearly there were certain dangers in auto racing. Drivers were always at risk, as were dogs, chickens, wandering cows, unsuspecting strollers, and inattentive spectators. This became apparent in the 1903 Paris to Madrid race when enthusiastic viewers crowded the course too closely and couldn't move away before being killed or injured. In all, there were nine fatalities, including driver Marcel Renault. The race was halted by French authorities at Bordeaux, and allowed to proceed no further. Afterwards, long distance road racing was moved to the closed circuit form, where it continues today at Grand Prix events like Le Mans.

THE NEW CENTURY AND GENERAL DEVELOPMENTS

At the turn of the twentieth century, America's motor vehicles still had the "horseless carriage" look and were powered by 1 or 2-cylinder engines. Within a few years a number of design changes began to take place; tillers were replaced by steering wheels, engines were moved from under the seat to the front of the vehicle, running boards were added, and larger, more powerful 4-cylinder engines began to replace the earlier ones. One could say that the "automobile" had at last arrived. In this new look, the "tonneau" body was added behind the front seat, providing extra seating. Made in carriage factories, these had either a side or rear door entrance. The carriage building industry was still strong at this time and traditional carriage styles, such as brougham, landaulet, phaeton, stanhope, and surrey were transferred to the automobile.

America's first National Automobile Show was held Nov. 3-10, 1900, in New York's

Madison Square Garden. On display were cars priced from less than $300 to more than $4,000. About 40 different companies showed their vehicles, and an obstacle course was set up to demonstrate them in action. The would-be-buyer could choose among gas, steam, and electric vehicles. Those preferring gas could then consider various transmission types, 2 versus 4-stroke engine cycles, and air versus water cooling.

In the horseless carriage days, people used bulb horns, whistles, and bells to give warning to traffic ahead. In the first decade of the twentieth century bulb horns were standard equipment on most automobiles. Later, as auto accessories became widely advertised, a number of sound devices were offered. These included horns, sirens, whistles, and even chimes. The first electric Klaxon horn, which produced the distinctive "ahoogha" sound, came out in 1908. Used in cars into the early 1930s, it became standard equipment on many. The first diaphragm type electric horn was invented by Oliver Lucas of Birmingham, England in 1910. This technology, much improved, is still used today in modern car horns.

A symbolic indicator of the new century's direction occurred on Jan. 10, 1901, when an oil-gusher came in at the Spindletop dome in Beaumont, Texas. This had the immediate effect of reducing oil prices as it began a longtime oil boom in Texas, that soon spread elsewhere. During the 20th century's first decade, entry into the automotive business was relatively easy. Most cars were assembled from parts that could be obtained on credit from many competing parts firms. Aside from an economic downturn or two, it was a high demand market and both dealers and buyers eagerly paid cash for new automobiles. A 60-day guarantee on new car purchases was approved by the 112-member National Association of Automobile Manufacturers in 1902. American automobile production was about 9,000 cars in 1902, 11,235 in 1903, and 22,130 in 1904.

In 1905, Charles J. Glidden, a telephone company magnate, initiated the Glidden Tour, an annual summer event that lasted through 1913. The first one was a run from New York City to New Hampshire's White Mountains and back, a distance of 870 miles. The winner was a Pierce Great Arrow, driven by Percy Pierce, son of the firm's owner. The 1906 tour covered a 1,500 mile distance and was also won by Mr. Pierce. Nineteen of the 48 cars entered finished the event.

Important metallurgical breakthroughs began around 1906. High-carbon steel, chrome-nickel steel, chrome-vanadium steel, and phosphor bronze were developed and adapted for automotive use. Aluminum alloys, which had been developed earlier, began to be used in automobiles at this time. In 1908, Cadillac offered the first car having entirely interchangeable parts. For this it was awarded Britain's Dewar Trophy for making the most outstanding contribution to the automotive industry.

In 1908, Edwin R. Thomas, maker of the Thomas Flyer automobile, entered a 4-cylinder, 60-hp touring car in the famous New York to Paris race, sponsored by the *New York Times* and the Parisian newspaper *Le Matin*. Thomas's lead driver was George Schuster. This was a very difficult contest as road conditions over much of the course were very poor, and sometimes—especially in Manchuria and Siberia—nonexistent. The other vehicles were a German Protos, an Italian Zust, and three French vehicles: a De Dion-Bouton, Motobloc, and Sizaire-Naudin. They left Times Square in New York on Feb. 12 on a course going through Chicago to San Francisco, then by ship to Valdez, Alaska, and then across the Bering Straits by ship to Asia.

Leading the race was the Thomas Flyer, which arrived in San Francisco in 41 days,

8 hours, and 15 minutes. It was the only one to reach Alaska, but impossible weather conditions allowed no further progress. So the race was rerouted through Japan to Vladivostok, Siberia. The Thomas team returned to Seattle, and then embarked for Japan. Only three contestants reached Vladivostok, and it was the same for Paris. The German Protos was first to arrive there on July 26th, but it was penalized for being shipped partway by rail. Arriving four days later was the Thomas Flyer, which was declared the winner.

In 1909, British Daimler began the first regular production of cars having the Knight Sleeve-Valve engine. Developed by the American Charles Yale Knight, it had been rejected in the U.S. and so he took it abroad. Sleeve-valves were quieter and required less maintenance than normal poppet-valves. But the Knight engines, which had two cast-iron sleeves per cylinder, were more expensive to build, had lubrication problems at higher speeds, tended to burn more oil than engines with poppet-valves, and were more difficult to start in cold weather.

Daimler's engineers made improvements to Knight's design before manufacturing it. It was thoroughly tested by the Royal Automobile Club and afterwards Daimler was awarded the 1909 Dewar Trophy. Once Daimler was on board it became easier to get other firms interested. Belgium's Minerva, France's Panhard et Levassor, and Germany's Mercedes were all subsequently licensed to use this technology. In 1911 the American firms of Stearns, Stoddard-Dayton, and Columbia received licensing, but unfortunately the latter two soon went bankrupt.

Whether or not it was stipulated in the licensing agreement, it became the custom in America that all car models using Knight engines would add the Knight name after their brand name. So over the years there were cars names like Atlas-Knight, Stearns-Knight, R&V Knight, Moline-Knight, Handley-Knight, Falcon-Knight, Lyons-Knight, and Willys-Knight. Willys made improvements to the Knight engine design before introducing its 4-cylinder Willys-Knight car in 1916. It introduced a 6-cylinder 60-hp model in 1925.

In its final 1930 model, Stearns-Knight built a straight-8, sleeve-valve engine generating 127-hp. Slide-valve engines first appeared in the U.S. with the 1924 Chrysler. They were very efficient and simpler than the sleeve-valve type. This technology was further improved by people like GM's Charles Kettering and Harry Ricardo. Willys-Knight became the last U.S. company to use the sleeve-valve, discontinuing production in the early 1930s. Daimler continued its use into the mid-1930s, and French production continued until the outbreak of World War II.

The Boyce Moto-Meter was introduced in 1912. Mounted atop the radiator cap, it showed the water temperature inside. Circular in shape, it had a thermometer running up its center and was built in a number of different styles into the late 1920s. By then cooling systems had improved, and some car firms replaced the Moto-Meter with a radiator cap ornament such as Lincoln's greyhound, Franklin's lion, and Pierce-Arrow's archer.

Philadelphia's Hale & Kilburn firm produced some steel auto body stampings for Hupp Motor Co. in 1912. The company's works manager, E.G. Budd had developed an all-steel rail car, and so his technology was applied for the first time to automobiles. In the beginning car bodies had been constructed almost entirely from wood, but later wood frameworks were covered with thin sheet metal. Budd subsequently left Hale & Kilburn to set up his own firm, the Edward G. Budd Manufacturing Co. in Philadelphia. He took orders from Oakland and Packard in 1913, and later became involved with Dodge Brothers in production of the first totally-welded, all-steel bodies. These were used for the company's first automobile, introduced for the 1915 model year.

IMPROVEMENTS IN TIRES & ROADS

The use of rubber tires was a result of the vulcanization process invented by Charles Goodyear in 1843. The pneumatic tire, invented in 1888 by John Dunlop, involved the use of an inner tube and was first used for bicycles. But in 1895 it was adapted by the Michelin brothers for motor carriages. However, both iron rimmed wooden wheels and solid rubber tires were used on some vehicles through the remainder of the century and likely beyond. Pneumatic technology was problematic for many years as drivers had to constantly deal with flats, blowouts, and short tire life. Thus it was essential to carry tire repair kits and extra tires. But over time a slow revolution took place as rubber became stronger and more flexible, cotton cord became the main base fabric, and more efficient tread designs were developed to improve traction.

Another innovation was the "demountable rim," whereby the rim could be removed from the wheel and replaced with another rim having an inflated tire. In this case spare rims were carried rather than spare wheels. Up to the 1920s, the shape of a tire's cross section was circular. But with the introduction of the low-pressure balloon tire the shape became elliptical. These tires were stronger and so a reduction of tire pressure to about 30 psi became possible. This resulted in a softer ride, longer tire life, and less wear to the highway.

Balloon tires became standard on most automobiles about 1925. About this same time welded metal spoke wheels replaced wooden spoke wheels, also improving the ride. Solid metal wheels had been introduced earlier, about 1920. The natural color of vulcanized rubber is white. For many years automobile tires were of this color, but later in the 1920s the tire industry began adding carbon black, resulting in the black tire. At this same time the white side-wall tire was developed as a luxury option.

In early-1900s rural America, there was considerable resistance to the idea of roadbuilding because it required raising property taxes. At the same time, however, the benefits of improved roads had become obvious, and so public opinion began to change. In 1907 the National Grange, a farmers' organization, and the American Automobile Association convened a Good Roads conference to consider possible legislation. Afterwards, a number of other Good Roads conventions were held, with a main goal being the establishment of a federal highway assistance program. Joining in this effort were a number of automotive industry organizations and the American Roadmakers' Association.

On Sep. 12, 1912, Carl G. Fisher, one of the investors in the Indianapolis Motor Speedway, suggested an intercontinental "coast to coast rock highway." His cause was taken up by Packard president Henry B. Joy, who suggested that the highway be dedicated as a monument to President Abraham Lincoln. A route of 3,389 miles through thirteen states was planned, starting at Times Square in New York and ending up at Lincoln Park in San Francisco. Prominent cities along the route included Philadelphia, Pittsburgh, Canton,

Fort Wayne, Joliet, Omaha, Cheyenne, and Salt Lake City. An official dedication of the "Lincoln Highway" took place on Oct. 31, 1913, and festivities were held at cities and towns all along the route.

However, at this time there wasn't much of a road connecting these cities. While the US had over two million miles of "roads" by then, the vast majority existed in rural areas and had no improvements of any kind. Improvements included grading and the use of various surfacing materials including oil, gravel, crushed rock, caliche, and crushed shells. Rarest of all were paved roads with brick, poured concrete, or asphalt surfaces. In 1928, when much of the Lincoln Highway officially became U.S. 30, it still remained a work in progress.

In 1914, Fisher became involved in planning the "Dixie Highway." Initially it was intended to run from Chicago to Miami. However, as objections were raised, an eastern route was added that began at Sault Ste. Marie, Michigan. Running parallel to the original road, it also terminated in Miami. Subsequently much of the eastern route became U.S. 25, and much of the western, U.S. 31.

While road building was under the aegis of cities and states, it received federal assistance for the first time after President Woodrow Wilson signed the Federal Aid Road Act of 1916. Under this act, $75 million was allocated for building roads on a matching fund arrangement. In order to qualify, a state was required to have a highway department. The Bureau of Public Roads was authorized to oversee things. Still a part of the U.S. Department of Agriculture, it had originally been established as the Office of Road Inquiry in 1893, became the Office of Public Roads in 1905, and in 1915 took on its present name. As this money was intended only for construction of rural post roads, the program received subsequent criticism for neglecting similar needs in urban areas.

1915 Oakland

Because of World War I, the Federal Aid Road Act of 1916 was never fully implemented. Under the Federal Aid Highway Act of 1921, the program was redirected toward developing a national highway system. In 1922, General John J. Pershing was commissioned to create the nation's first official topographic road map. It was later used by the agency in establishing road building priorities. By the end of 1921, all of the $75 million had been disbursed and by 1923 all of the authorized roads had been built. America in 1924 had 31,000 miles of paved roads. Beginning with Oregon in 1919, states started taxing gas sales to raise road building funds, and in the next decade all the other states followed.

In 1925 there were over 250 different "named" roads, including the Lincoln and Dixie highways, and another transcontinental route, the Bankhead Highway, that ran from Washington, DC to San Diego. Each had its distinctive markers placed along the routes which often created confusion for drivers. That year the American Association of State Highway Officials (AASHO) and Bureau of Public Roads began designing a coherent road numbering system for U.S. highways. The result, approved Nov. 11, 1926, set rules whereby east-west routes were assigned even numbers and north-south roads odd numbers. Lowest numbers for north-south routes began in the east and became higher farther west. Lowest numbers for east-west roads began in the north and became higher farther south.

THE ERA OF THE ELECTRIC CAR

The electric automobile had one brief moment of glory on the racetrack when it set a famous speed record. This happened near Paris on Apr. 29, 1899 when Belgian Camille Jenatzy became the first person to drive a road vehicle at 100-kilometers per hour (62 mph). He did this in his torpedo-shaped battery-powered racer, "Jamais Contente." Electric vehicle brands introduced in America that year included Baker Electric, Cleveland (1899-1916); Crowdus Electric, Chicago (1899-1902). and Woods Electric, Chicago (1899-1918).

Electric vehicles had certain advantages over their gas-powered counterparts. They didn't have to be started, and without having clutch and gearbox, they were much simpler to operate. The driver only had to twist the control handle, steer with a tiller, and away she or he went. Electrics were cleaner and quieter, they expelled no exhaust fumes, and had no cooling system to worry about. The best year for electric vehicle sales was 1900, when they totaled 38 percent of the market, but by 1905 this figure had plummeted below 7 percent. However as late as 1914 new electric car makers entered the market.

Because of their silence and simple operation electrics appeared to find favor with women. Electric car advertising became almost exclusively directed towards them. In the early 1900s, electric stanhopes, surreys, victorias, runabouts, and roadsters were produced. From about 1910 into the late-1920s electric vehicles were mainly elegant-looking coupes, coaches, and broughams, with comfortable interiors, fine upholstery, and sometimes large curved-glass windows and curtains. These had enough headroom to accommodate the large hats fashionable with women for a time. Prices of electrics then were mainly in the $1,500-$4,000 range. In this period, driving was typically done from the back seat. Often there was an informal arrangement of the seats and sometimes front seats were faced backwards. Bicycle-type wheels were sometimes used as they provided a softer ride than the wooden spoke variety.

Batteries were placed in the front of the vehicle and the electric motor in back. Unfortunately, it was battery-power that was the weak link in this technology. Storage batteries were made with lead plates. They were heavy and expensive, and although they could be recharged, they deteriorated quickly. Designing these vehicles became a balancing act between having as much battery capacity as possible on one hand, and not having too much weight on the other. This resulted in a limited cruising range, making these vehicles impractical for rural use. Thus they were mainly driven on paved roads in urban areas; typically operated at low speeds.

By 1920, large hats had gone out of style, and so for the most part, had electrics. A few firms held on for awhile, but the Detroit Electric was the final survivor, amazingly lasting to 1939. About 1930 the company made some radical styling changes. The tiller was replaced with a steering wheel, headroom was reduced, the seating setup became conventional, and with the help of a faux radiator, the Detroit Electric looked like an average gas car. Production in the 1930s was mainly 4-passenger coupes with two wheelbase sizes.

Among America's many electric vehicle brands were the following: Ajax Electric, New York (1901-03); Buffalo Electric, Buffalo (1901-06); Studebaker Electric, South Bend, Indiana (1902-12); Columbus Electric, Columbus, Ohio (1903-15); Pope-Waverly Electric, Indianapolis (1904-08); Rauch & Lang Electric, Cleveland (1905-1920) and Chicopee Falls, Massachusetts (1920-28); Babcock Electric, Buffalo (1906-12); Detroit Electric, Detroit (1907-1939); Bailey Electric, Amesbury, Massachusetts (1907-16); Borland Electric, Chicago (1910-14); Hupp-Yeats Electric, Detroit (1911-19); Chicago Electric, Chicago (1912-16); and Milburn Electric, Toledo (1914-23).

THE ELECTRIC CAB VENTURE & THE SELDEN PATENT

Rochester patent lawyer, George B. Selden, had received his patent for a gas-powered road engine on Nov. 5, 1895. Apparently, he did nothing with it until he sold it to a group of Wall Street investors in 1899 for $10,000 and 20 percent of future royalties collected. This group, headed by financier William Collins Whitney and Thomas F. Ryan, planned on manufacturing fleets of electric taxis and operating them in major American cities. In early 1899 they acquired Isaac L. Rice's Electric Vehicle Co., which produced the hansom cabs that had begun operating in New York and Philadelphia. Having bigger plans, they then approached Pope Manufacturing Co. in Hartford, with the intent of acquiring the firm's automotive manufacturing facilities.

After complex negotiations this was arranged and Columbia Automobile Co. emerged, completely separating from Pope's enterprise. Columbia would build electric hansom cabs but also continue production of Hiram Maxim's gasoline vehicles. Electric

Vehicle Co., which now controlled Columbia, would function as a holding company, setting up subsidiary taxi operations in various cities. After about 2,000 cabs were built, however, it was found that their operation was too expensive. As this venture collapsed, Electric Vehicle became known in the media as "the Lead Cab Trust." Desperate for cash, the partners turned to the Selden Patent, demanding royalty payments from all American gas car producers.

In 1900 Winton and certain other firms were sued for patent infringement. This led to negotiations which in 1903 established the Association of Licensed Automobile Manufacturers (ALAM). This organization acquired control of the patent, and an executive committee of five (with Electric Vehicle Co. as permanent member) was established to oversee licensing operations. The royalty established was 1.25 percent of the list price of each car manufactured. Of the total royalties collected 40 percent went to Electric Vehicle, 40 percent to ALAM, and 20 percent to George B. Selden.

ALAM was supposed to use its money for the benefit of the industry. One of its efforts was to establish a technical section with the intent of standardizing parts and materials industrywide. Apparently some attempt was also made to eliminate "fly by night" car producers, but the organization also became a kind of exclusive club. One problem of this arrangement was that newcomers to the business were left in an awkward situation. On one hand, they weren't supposed to manufacture gasoline cars without a license, but on the other they could only receive a license after they had demonstrated a capacity for building vehicles meeting association standards. Even George B. Selden encountered this dilemma when he started producing cars in Rochester in 1908. His license request was refused and his operation only became legal the following year when he purchased a defunct company having the license.

When Henry Ford began building his first version of the Model A in 1903 he made an attempt to acquire a license but was rebuffed. Deciding to fight, he refused to recognize the legality of the patent. Soon other manufacturers, Ransom E. Olds among them, joined in this effort, and formed a counter organization, The American Motor Car Manufacturers Association (AMCMA). At its inception it had more members than ALAM.

The result was a court battle lasting for eight years. To test the validity of Selden's patented plan, two vehicles were constructed from his original 1879 specifications. By the barest margin his plan was accepted as valid. In 1909 the district court decided in favor of ALAM, causing the immediate breakup of AMCMA. However, this ruling was appealed and in 1911 the Circuit Court of Appeals ruled in Ford's favor. It found that Selden's patent only applied to a two-stroke engine of the Brayton type. Thus the patent was valid, but not infringed.

As it was, the Selden Patent was due to expire in 1912 anyway, but winning the case saved Ford and other firms from paying large sums in back royalties. ALAM was dissolved, and subsequently replaced by the National Automobile Chamber of Commerce. In 1901, Electric Vehicle Co. had assumed sponsorship of Columbia car production, dropping the Columbia Automobile Co. name. During the panic of 1907, Electric Vehicle went into receivership, remaining in a precarious state afterwards. It changed its name to Columbia Motor Car Co. in 1909. Afterwards it became a part of George Briscoe's United States Motors, but dropped production in 1913.

COL. POPE'S AUTOMOBILE EMPIRE

Col. Albert A. Pope had been involved in manufacturing for decades and operated on a large scale. He created his American Bicycle Co., known as the "bicycle trust" in the late 1890s. An umbrella organization, it controlled nearly 50 different firms selling bicycles under their own names. However, the bicycle era was ending, and a stock surplus resulted in intense price competition. Pope had sold off his promising Columbia Automobile Co. in 1899, but he soon decided to get back into the game.

In September 1900, American Bicycle announced that it was going to use its factory in Toledo, Ohio for making steam cars. Reorganized as the International Motor Car Co., it introduced two models, the Toledo and the Westchester in early 1901. Subsequently all new models were marketed under the Toledo name. In 1902, International introduced a 3-cylinder, 16-hp gasoline vehicle. In 1903, it offered two more gasoline models but eliminated a steam car.

On May 27, 1903, International was reorganized as the Pope Motor Car Co. of Toledo. Its new automobile, the Pope-Toledo, would be introduced for the 1904 model year. These were well-made vehicles, and in November 1903 a stock 4-cylinder, 24-hp car was raced on the West Coast, winning most of its events. The list price for this automobile was $3,500. The company also offered a 2-cylinder, 14-hp model for $2,000. From 1905 to its demise in 1909, the company only offered 4-cylinder models. After 1905 these branched from tonneau types into landaulets, limousines, runabouts, and touring cars, including some with a Victoria top.

Among the various Pope brands, the Pope-Toledo was the finest. Unfortunately, after the financial panic of 1907 Pope's empire fell into serious disarray. Pope-Toledo went into bankruptcy in 1908, but under receivership production of the 1909 models continued into January. The factory was sold in April of that year to the Willys-Overland company.

In the summer of 1902, Col. Pope acquired the Robinson Motor Vehicle Co. of Hyde Park, Massachusetts. While John T. Robinson was retained as president, Col. Pope's nephew, Edward W. Pope became secretary-treasurer. The company's 1903 Pope-Robinson was larger than its predecessor. It was a high quality product, having a 4-cylinder, 24-hp T-head engine that could reach 35 mph. Unfortunately, at $6,000 it was priced too high. The price was reduced to $4,500 in 1904 but sales were not good and Mr. Robinson became ill, passing away that November. Production was halted and the company was sold to Buick, allowing it to acquire the firm's ALAM license.

In 1903, Pope Manufacturing Co. of Hartford began developing a 1-cylinder prototype car. Introduced as the Pope-Hartford in 1904, it was followed by a 2-cylinder model in 1905, and a 4-cylinder car in 1906. While runabout and tonneau models were produced the first two years, a touring car was offered in 1906, and in 1907, a limousine. In 1911, a 6-cylinder, 50-hp model was added. Company prices then ranged from a $3,000 4-cylinder touring car to a $5,150 6-cylinder limousine or landaulet.

Col. Pope passed away on Aug. 10, 1909, and his brother George assumed control. The company was in difficult circumstances and went through three receiverships, the last one in 1913. Production continued into 1914 before halting. The factory was sold to Pratt

& Whitney early the next year. One of the criticisms of the company was that it offered too many models considering the small number of vehicles it produced.

The Crawford Bicycle factory in Hagerstown, Maryland, was taken over for production of the Pope-Tribune car. This vehicle was intended to be smaller and cheaper; providing some low-end options for Pope customers. Col. Pope's son, Harold, was put in charge of operations. For 1904 a 1-cylinder, 6-hp runabout was offered at $650. A 2-cylinder, 12-hp tonneau was added in 1905 for $900. For 1906 the 2-cylinder car was offered in runabout and touring models, both selling for $900.

Pope-Tribune's sole offering in 1907 was a 4-cylinder vehicle, priced at $1,750 in both runabout and touring models. After that year's financial panic, Pope-Tribune went into receivership. Despite this, for the 1908 model year, the firm kept its previous models at the same price, and added a larger 4-cylinder car at $2,750. In switching from a cheap product into the mid-range, Pope-Tribune may have lost its customer base and raison d'etre. Production halted and the factory was sold that November.

The Waverly Electric was produced at Indiana Bicycle's factory in Indianapolis. It had come into being in 1898 through a merger between Chicago's American Electric Vehicle Co. and Indiana Bicycle. The Waverly enterprise was absorbed into American Bicycle Co. in 1900, and fell under the sponsorship of Pope's International Motor Car Co. It was reorganized as the Pope Motor Car Co. of Indianapolis in 1904, its product becoming the Pope-Waverly Electric. Operations were expanded, resulting in a wider range of models. In 1907 the company went into receivership, with production continuing into 1908. The factory was sold that September to a local group, who resumed production under the Waverly name. They continued in business to 1916.

HENRY FORD, THE MODEL T, LINCOLN, AND THE MODEL A

Born July 30, 1863, on a Michigan farm, Henry Ford showed an early inclination towards mechanical things. He moved to Detroit at age 16 and gained experience working in machine shops for almost a decade. He married Clara Jane Bryant in 1888, and took a job as an engineer with Edison Illuminating Co. in 1891. On the side, Ford began testing a gasoline engine in his home. This led to his 2-cylinder, 4-hp "Quadricycle," first tested in Detroit on June 4, 1896. Famously, Ford's vehicle had been built in a small shed, and after completion there wasn't sufficient door space for its removal. So a part of the shed wall was ripped out to facilitate matters.

Ford's experimental efforts continued and began to attract local attention. In 1899, he was approached by a group of wealthy Detroit businessmen, including mayor William C. Maybury. This resulted in creation of the Detroit Automobile Co., with Ford as superintendent. Ford's first decision was to build a racer, which in 1901 beat a Winton at Grosse Pointe racing track. The firm was reorganized as the Henry Ford Co. on Nov. 30, 1901, but early the next year his backers turned against him because he seemed more intent on racing cars than producing them. Intent on divesting themselves, they brought in Henry Leland, a partner in a prominent machine shop, to give an appraisal. Ford reacted angrily and quickly resigned. Leland showed them a prototype engine he had built and suggested that they continue with their effort. Subsequently this venture was reorganized as Cadillac Automobile Co., and soon Leland became its president.

Ford's interest in racing continued and he built two racers, the "Arrow" and "999." The latter vehicle became quite famous when, at Grosse Pointe in June 1903, it set a record, by becoming the first racer to circle a one-mile track in less than a minute. It had a monstrous 4-cylinder, 1,155.3 cubic-inch engine. Its driver, Barney Oldfield, a novice at the time, acquired instant celebrity, and afterwards had a brilliant career. For decades after his early triumphs, many a speeding driver was addressed by a policeman as a "regular Barney Oldfield."

With the backing of Alexander Young Malcomson, a coal magnate, Ford Motor Co. was established on June, 16, 1903. Just a month later, Ford was turning out his 2-cylinder, 8-hp Model A car. With the engine mounted under the seat, it was available in runabout and tonneau models, priced at $850 and $950, respectively. The 2-cylinder, 10-hp Model C, which followed in late 1904, had the fuel tank placed in the front under a hood. Also brought out that year was the shaft-driven 4-cylinder, 24-hp Model B, priced at $2,000. A 4-passenger touring car with brass trim, it had a front-mounted engine and could reach a top speed of 40 mph. In February 1905 Ford introduced his 2-cylinder, 16-hp Model F. It was available in touring car and coupe models.

Later in 1905 the 6-cylinder, 40-hp Model K made its debut. It gained fame for the company when it broke a world 24-hour driving record, covering a distance of 1,135 miles while averaging 47.2 mph. Apparently, however, Ford didn't like building expensive cars like his Models B and K. This had been done at the behest of Malcomson. So around this time he bought out his partner, gaining more flexibility for himself in charting the company's future. Also introduced in 1905 was the 4-cylinder, 15-18-hp Model N, priced at $500. In February 1906, the Model R made its appearance and in 1907, the Model S. These were essentially further refinements of the Model N. Ford sales for 1907 were 14,887 cars, placing it first in the industry.

Henry Ford's side-valve, 4-cylinder, 20-hp Model T was first advertised on Oct. 3, 1908 in the *Saturday Evening Post*. It was to become America's most famous automobile. Intended for mass consumption, it was relatively cheap, durable, easy to operate and maintain, and simple enough mechanically for the owner to make most repairs. Having 30-inch wheels, a semi-elliptical spring mounted transverely for each of the front and rear beam axles, and a high-mounted body, it was ideal for country roads.

The Model T was the natural outcome of Ford's practical, disciplined, and persistent nature; his engineering and managerial genius; and the able assistance of some very good engineers. Among these was Childe Harold Wills, a metallurgist who conducted experiments with vanadium steel. His efforts resulted in lighter and stronger parts, used throughout most of the vehicle, giving it the rugged qualities it became known for.

Widely known as the "Tin-Lizzie" or "Flivver," the Model T was basic but very well built, and priced far below any vehicle of comparable quality. Among its features was a 2-speed planetary transmission, an engine cast in one block with a detachable cylinder head, and a magneto built into the flywheel for providing ignition current. It also had left-side steering, leather upholstery, and, to assist operations it had three pedal controls and two levers. The right foot pedal operated the Model T's main brake, applying a band on a drum in the transmission. Low speed and reverse were likewise bands on the gear drums of the transmission. There was no gas pedal, only the hand throttle. The big lever on the left did three things; full forward was "go," straight up was neutral, and all the way back was "parking brake." It was surprisingly simple to learn, and clutching was easy.

The Model T could reach a top speed of 45 mph and its fuel consumption was about 25 mpg. Having brass radiator and lamps, it was initially offered in runabout, touring car, coupe, landaulet, and town car models. These were priced at $825, $850, $950, $950, and $1,000, respectively. The bodies of these vehicles were all made from wood, and they were offered in three colors, gray, red, and green (until 1913). After about 2,500 cars were built, Ford made some changes and began a standardization process. This was the case with the Model T from then on, as it subsequently went through many adjustments and changes until its demise in 1927.

In 1909 Ford dropped production of all previous models, and concentrated solely on the Model T. In 1913 the company added front doors to its touring cars and instituted a policy where black became the only color option. Mass production of the Model T began at Ford's Highland Park factory in August 1913, with a moving line for final chassis assembly. By January 1914, final assembly time had been cut from 12.5 hours to 1 hour and 33 minutes. About that same time Ford reduced daily work hours from 9 to 8 and increased daily pay to $5.00, almost doubling the industry standard. This was done at the behest of James S. Couzens, the business manager, who was concerned about high employee turnover. This change had the desired result and greatly improved worker morale—and retention.

In 1914 Ford built 300,000 vehicles while the rest of the industry manufactured approximately 200,000. Mass production and the resultant economies of scale gave Ford a tremendous competitive advantage, and Model T prices were subsequently reduced, reaching a low point of $290 in 1924. In 1915, the Model T acquired electric lights, and on the 1917 model, a black radiator replaced the brass one. In 1919, an electric starter became optional for the Model T. In 1922, annual Ford sales exceeded one million for the first time. Balloon tires were added in 1925, followed the next year by a nickel-plated radiator and a number of color options.

In May 1926, Model T production reached a total of 15 million cars. Over the years it had been assembled in a number of American cities and in several foreign countries. However, by the mid 1920s it had become dated. Competing companies like Chevrolet were offering better engineered, more attractive cars with a wider range of options. While Ford was very attached to his Model T, he was finally persuaded by his son, Edsel, and company managers to give it up. Production halted at the end of May, 1927.

In 1922, Henry Ford bought Lincoln Motor Co. from Henry M. Leland and his son for $8 million. It is interesting that Leland had taken the wreck of Ford's first company and turned it into Cadillac, staying at its helm to 1917. Cadillac was a part of General Motors then, and Leland and his GMC chief, William C. Durant, had a dispute, resulting in Leland's departure. The disagreement was over manufacture of the Liberty aircraft engine for wartime needs, which Leland wanted to undertake, but which at the time Durant opposed. Upon leaving, the Lelands set up Lincoln Motor Co. to do just that. But the war's end came before production was fully set up, and the Lelands moved on to designing an automobile.

The Model L Lincoln, which first appeared in September 1920, was a precision-made machine. It was powered by an 81-hp, 60-degree V-8 engine. Having a top speed of 70 mph, it was intended to sell in the $5,000 price range. However, its exterior styling was somewhat dated, and its arrival time, unfortunately, coincided with the full onset of the postwar recession. The Lelands decided to solve the styling problem with help from Buffalo's Brunn coachwork firm, but low sales figures prompted Lincoln's board of directors to scuttle these plans. Instead, they put the company into receivership and offered it for sale.

Under Ford's ownership it was intended that the Lelands would stay on, but they left four months later. Edsel Ford, Ford's president at the time, apparently was very involved with Lincoln. Despite Leland fears to the contrary, Lincoln engineering and styling were steadily improved, and the company quickly became profitable. Series production began for some beautiful models designed by major coach building firms like Brunn, Judkins, Dietrich, and LeBaron. The stylish greyhound radiator ornament was added in 1928, and the Model L of 1929 could reach speeds of 90 mph. In 1931 it was replaced by the elegantly designed Model K. Initially it was powered by a 120-hp V-8 engine, but in 1932 a 150-hp V-12 became available.

Ford's greatly anticipated Model A was introduced on Dec. 2, 1927. It had a flat-head, 4-cylinder, 40-hp engine, and featured a 3-speed sliding gear transmission and 4-wheel brakes. It was a pronounced improvement over the 20-hp Model T with its 2-speed planetary transmission and 2-wheel brakes. Model A styling apparently drew inspiration from Lincoln designs, but was more compact. The initial models were priced between $460 and $600, and were produced at Ford's massive River Rouge factory.

During the six-month production shutdown in 1927, Ford had lost its position as sales leader to Chevrolet. In the Model A's 1928-31 sales period, the two companies were very close competitors, with Ford leading in 1929 and 1930, and Chevrolet ahead in 1928 and 1931. Almost 5 million Model A cars were built before it was replaced in early 1932 with Ford's famous 65-hp, flat head, V-8 model. Ford Motor Co. and its Lincoln subsidiary survived the Great Depression and continue with us today. Its Mercury automobile division was started in 1938, but shut down in early 2011. Ford's short-lived Edsel car was built from 1958-60. Henry Ford, the man who started it all, passed away on Apr. 7, 1947.

RANSOM E. OLDS, OLDSMOBILE AND REO

Ransom Eli Olds, born in Geneva, Ohio, on June 3, 1864, had a longtime interest in self-propelled vehicles, and early on had built a couple of steam carriages. In 1896 he built a 1-cylinder, 5-hp, 4-passenger gas-powered vehicle, and soon followed it with several more. At this time he was involved in his family business, P.F. Olds & Son Co., a thriving manufacturer of gasoline engines. Wanting to keep his new operation separate, he established the Olds Motor Vehicle Co. in Lansing, Michigan, on Aug. 21, 1897. His initial vehicles were of a simple design, having a 1-cylinder motor, tiller steering, and 2-speed planetary transmission. This business was moving very slowly until he gained the backing of Samuel L. Smith, a lumber tycoon. This enabled Olds to reorganize his separate businesses into the Olds Motor Works in Detroit on May 8, 1899. Two of Smith's sons joined the firm and Olds began working on new vehicle designs.

In the spring of 1901 a fire destroyed most of the factory, and of eleven experimental models only one was saved. It became the prototype of the curved-dash runabout, later made famous in a popular song, "In My Merry Oldsmobile." Acting quickly to save his firm, Olds approached various Detroit parts suppliers, and gathering the necessary materials, managed to build 425 vehicles before the year's end. Priced at $650, these featured a 1-cylinder, 7-hp, 4-stroke engine, 2-speed all-spur geared transmission, and center chain drive.

A peripheral but interesting part of this story is that Olds went to the firm of Leland & Faulconer to produce his engine. Henry Leland, one of the firm's partners and a precision machinery expert, suggested some design changes for improving power, and created a motor to show Olds. Olds, however, was very busy then and, not wanting to delay production further, had the motors built as originally ordered. In 1902, Leland brought along his improved engine when he was consulted regarding the ailing Henry Ford Co. Soon afterwards the firm was reorganized as the Cadillac Automobile Co., and Leland's motor became the prototype for its first engines.

In 1902, Olds became the first in the industry to use assembly line production. Requiring interchangeable parts, this method was pioneered in 1802 by Marc Isambard Brunel at England's Portsmouth Block Mills. Its first American use was in 1821 when Thomas Blanchard employed it for arms manufacture at Springfield Armory in Springfield, Massachusetts. Essential for mass production on any scale, this practice speeds up assembly, resulting in greater worker productivity and economies of scale.

Annual production figures were 2,500 in 1902, 4,000 in 1903, 5,508 in 1904, and 6,500 in 1905. Oldsmobile moved back to Lansing in 1904, but that January Olds left the firm after quarreling with the Smiths over Oldsmobile's future direction. They wanted to make more expensive vehicles while Olds wanted to build models for the general public. The Smiths got their way, but production of the curved-dash runabout continued through 1907.

That year Oldsmobile also offered three 4-cylinder cars powered by a 35 to 40-hp engine. These were the Model H Flying Roadster priced at $2,750, the Model A 5-passenger Touring Car priced at $2,750, and the Model A Limousine priced at $3,800. Despite declining sales, the company's 1908 6-cylinder Model Z was introduced in the summer, a $4,200 touring car. The Panic of 1907, which arrived in October, dropped stock market prices by almost 50 percent and set off a recession. Left in a precarious spot, Oldsmobile was purchased in late 1908 by William C. Durant's General Motors Corporation.

Under General Motors management, Oldsmobile was resuscitated. A new 1909 offering was the $1,250 4-cylinder Model 20. Essentially a makeover of the Buick Model 10, it accounted for 5,325 of 6,575 Oldsmobiles sold that year. However, it was discontinued for 1910 and Oldsmobile introduced its 4-cylinder Special Series and 6-cylinder Limited Series. The former were priced from $3,000 to $4,200, and the latter luxury models priced from $4,600 to $5,800. In 1911, Oldsmobile introduced its 4-cylinder Autocrat Series. Filling the gap between the Specials and Limiteds, these cars were priced from $3,500 to $5,000. Oldsmobile's most expensive car then was its 7-passenger Limited Limousine priced at $7,000.

The 4-cylinder Defender Series, which replaced the Special Series in 1912, took the firm in a different direction. Over the next several years, Oldsmobile moved out of the luxury market into mid-range competition. In 1914-15, the 4-cylinder Model 42 Baby Olds Series was offered. By 1915 company prices ran from $1,285 to $2,975. In 1916 Oldsmobile introduced its Light Eight Series, powered by a 40-hp, V-8 engine. From then through 1923 the company offered a choice of 4, 6, and 8-cylinder vehicles. However, from 1924 through 1931, only 6-cylinder models were offered. In 1929, Oldsmobile introduced the 81-hp Viking V-8 as its companion car but it only lasted until 1930. Production high points were 22,613 units in 1917, 44,854 in 1924, 86,593 in 1928, and over 100,000 in 1929.

Having left Oldsmobile in 1904, Ransom E. Olds formed the Reo Motor Car Co. in Lansing that summer. The letters in Reo were the initials of Olds' name. The first Reo was completed in mid-October and was test driven for 2,000 miles. A 2-cylinder, 16-hp 5-passenger Tonneau, it was introduced at the New York Automobile Show in January 1905. Olds soon added a 1-cylinder 7.5-hp Runabout, and in 1906 a 4-cylinder 24-hp Touring Car. These vehicles were priced at $1,250, $650, and $2,500 respectively.

Two Reo cross-country runs were made in 1905, and Reo vehicles were entered in other endurance tests. Reo cars quickly gained popularity and in 1907 reached third place in national sales, trailing only Ford and Buick. Following Ford's 1908 introduction of the Model T, Reo responded the next year with a 4-cylinder, 35-hp car priced at $1,250. It had a 226 cu. in. F-head engine, shaft drive, multiple disc clutch, left-side steering, and a worm & sector type steering gear. In 1912, Olds introduced his 4-cylinder "Reo the Fifth," which he called his farewell car. Its primary improvement over previous models was a center gearshift control. After this Olds turned most of the operation over to his managers but remained involved in key decisions.

In 1916, the company introduced a 6-cylinder 45-hp model. During the war years Reo was heavily involved in truck manufacture. In 1920, the company introduced its 6-cylinder, 50-hp, F-head T-6 model. Offered in several body styles, it was priced from $1,650 to $2,400. The 6-cylinder, 65-hp Reo Flying Cloud appeared in 1927, with body styling by Fabio Segardi. That same year Reo's 6-cylinder, 50-hp companion car, the Wolverine, was introduced. However its production only lasted two years.

Reo's finest car was its 8-cylinder, 125-hp Royale, built from 1931-34. It was elegantly styled and had a beautiful interior. Weakened by the Great Depression, Reo halted car production in 1936, but continued truck manufacture until 1967. That year it was merged with Diamond T, becoming the Diamond Reo Trucks Division of White Motor Corporation. Ransom E. Olds passed away in Lansing, Michigan, on Aug. 25, 1950.

BUICK, WILLIAM C. DURANT, AND GENERAL MOTORS

David Dunbar Buick, born in Scotland on Sep. 17, 1854, was a Detroit plumbing company owner who developed a process for bonding porcelain to cast iron. Subsequently he became known for creating the first white bathtubs. In 1899 he sold off his firm and started to manufacture gasoline engines, first calling his enterprise Buick Auto-Vim and

Power Co. This company became Buick Motor Co. in 1902. Buick was joined by Walter Marr and Eugene Richard, a former Olds employee, and together they developed a valve-in-head engine. In 1903 they built and tested their first automobile.

Backing this enterprise was Benjamin Briscoe, a sheet metal manufacturer who acquired a 97 percent interest in the firm. However, Briscoe became unhappy with the slow progress at Buick, and later that year passed off the operation to James H. Whiting of Flint Wagon Works in Flint, Michigan. Unfortunately, progress remained slow, with Buick's first car sale only coming in August 1904. By then Whiting was running out of capital, so on Nov. 1, 1904, William Crapo (Billy) Durant, a partner in the Durant-Dort Carriage Co., acquired Buick.

Durant had been born in Boston on Dec. 8, 1861. He was both likeable and aggressive, and had a reputation for being a master salesman. Within a year he increased Buick's capital stock from $75,000 to $1,500,000. Enos DeWalters, a former employee of Thomas and Cadillac, joined the engineering staff in 1905. David Buick apparently became less important to the firm and was gone by the end of 1908. The 1904-06 Buick cars (Models B, C, F, and G) had a 2-cylinder, 21 to 22-hp engine and 2-speed planetary transmission. They were first offered only as touring cars, with a runabout added in 1906. These were priced that year at $1,250 and $1,150 respectively. Buick sales in 1906 were 1,400 cars, placing it eighth in in the industry. The following year 4,641 cars were sold and the firm ranked second. Introduced for 1907 was Buick's T-head, 4-cylinder, 30-hp Model D. From then through 1911 a number of 2- and 4-cylinder models were offered.

Durant at this time was not only operating Buick, but was attempting to realize a larger vision. Perhaps inspired by Col. Pope, he saw the potential for a large company offering automobiles covering the whole spectrum of price options. In 1907, he and Benjamin Briscoe tried to unite four major companies: Buick, Maxwell-Briscoe, Ford, and Reo. But Ford and Reo demanded cash and the deal fell through. Going his separate way, Durant established General Motors Holding Co. in 1908. He acquired Oldsmobile that year, and also Oakland, adding Cadillac in 1909. However he had bought up other companies that, aside from eliminating some competition, proved to be poor investments.

Durant was almost immediately overextended. Yielding to the demands of a banking syndicate headed by James J. Storrow, he agreed to leave GM in exchange for sufficient loans to keep the company afloat. However, he did manage to have his Durant-Dort general manager, Charles W. Nash, take over the helm at Buick. In November 1912, Nash became GM president, and Walter P. Chrysler succeeded him at Buick. Earlier that year the first GMC Truck models appeared. This GM subsidiary resulted from the merger of the Rapid and Reliance truck firms which Durant had acquired in 1909.

Introduced in 1911 was Buick's first closed car, a 5-passenger limousine priced at $2,750. Only 4-cylinder vehicles were offered in 1912-13, but Buick's first 6-cylinder car, the 48-hp Model B-55, was introduced in 1914. It was almost a foot longer than previous Buicks. That year company prices ranged from $950 to $1,985. In 1916, production reached 124,834 vehicles, placing Buick third behind Ford and Willys-Overland. Replacing Walter Chrysler in 1920 was Harry H. Bassett, who kept the Buick helm to 1926. In 1924, Buick added 4-wheel brakes, detachable cylinder heads, and Packard-like styling on its radiator shell and hood. Buick discontinued 4-cylinder models the next year, offering only six-cylinder cars through 1930.

For the 1930 model year, Buick introduced its companion car, the 6-cylinder Marquette. Unlike Buick's valve-in-head engine, the Marquette had an L-head. While having some Buick features, the exterior also incorporated elements of Oldsmobile styling. However, because of the rapidly deepening Great Depression, production lasted just one year. In 1931, Buick upgraded from an all 6-cylinder lineup to all 8-cylinder cars. Today it remains a very successful company. After leaving the company named after him, David Dunbar Buick involved himself in two failed automotive ventures. Impoverished at the end, he passed away on Mar. 5, 1929.

After William Durant left General Motors in 1910, he returned to Flint and established the Little Motor Car Co., selling 3,500 4-cylinder, 20-hp roadsters in 1912. Priced at $690, this cheaply built car was also sold in 1913 along with a six-cylinder model, but production for both stopped at the end of May. Previously, while running Buick, Durant had been involved in racing. One of his best drivers was Swiss-born Louis Chevrolet. After leaving GM, Durant collaborated with his former driver and in 1911 they formed Chevrolet Motor Co. Backing Durant at this time was the Canadian R.S. McLaughlin, with whom Durant did business for many years. Chevrolet was put to work designing a car and the first model appeared in late 1912. The Chevrolet Six Type C Classic had an overhead valve, T-head, 299 cubic inch engine. Offered only as a touring car it was priced at $2,250. It was well built, but heavy, and didn't sell well.

In 1914, Durant bought Chevrolet out and he left to build another car. Durant worked to synthesize the Chevrolet and Little vehicles into a good quality but relatively cheap Chevrolet. In the meantime, he worked out a scheme with the Du Pont family to create a holding company, Chevrolet Motors Co. of Delaware, to absorb Michigan-based Chevrolet Motor Co. Durant then began offering five shares of Chevrolet stock for one share of General Motors stock. GM at the time had some disgruntled stockholders because it was paying no dividends. By this method Durant and the Duponts acquired enough GM stock to take over the company in 1916.

Once Durant was back in charge, Charles Nash left, and in 1917 the Lelands left Cadillac. Nash, with the help of banker James J. Storrow, bought out the Thomas B. Jeffery Co. of Kenosha, Wisconsin. Jeffrey had previously built the Rambler but at this time was building the Jeffery car. After Nash's takeover these vehicles continued in production for a time, becoming the first Nash automobiles.

In 1918, General Motors Corporation was formed; absorbing General Motors Holding Co., Chevrolet, and United Motors Corporation. The latter was another Durant project, composed of various parts manufacturers. Among these were Delco and Hyatt Roller Bearing Co. From them, Charles F. Kettering and Alfred P. Sloan, respectively, rose to become prominent GM players, with Sloan becoming GM vice-president in 1918.

In 1919, GM acquired Fisher Body Co., the world's largest car body manufacturer, run by the seven Fisher brothers. About this same time it purchased the refrigerator firm Frigidaire, and began General Motors Acceptance Co. (GMAC) for providing loans to car customers. While Durant made some good choices, he also made some mistakes. The worst was a decision to compete with Henry Ford's Fordson Tractor, a venture that cost GM $30 million. To do this GM purchased a California-based tractor firm and moved its operation to Janesville, Wisconsin. Then valuable time was expended making plans and setting up production. GM's Samson Model M Tractor emerged as the post-war recession was beginning. It was a good product but Ford quickly cut prices to the point where GM could no longer compete.

In his book *The American Automobile: A Brief History*, John B. Rae sums up GM's situation at this time:

> The trouble was that there was no co-ordination of the sprawling General Motors structure. William C. Durant was a man of tremendous dynamism and drive, but he either could not or would not concentrate on keeping the affairs of General Motors in order. He swung irregularly between ignoring his subordinates and interfering with them, and much of his time and effort was devoted to stock market operations. He was estimated to have had at least seventy separate brokerage accounts. Chrysler stood it until early in 1920 when the farm machinery fiasco proved too much for him and he quit. Sloan, also disturbed by the mismanagement, or rather non-management of the company, submitted a reorganization plan to Durant at this time, basically the one he himself was to apply later. Durant approved the plan but did nothing about it. Sloan then took a trip to Europe to think things over. He decided to resign when he returned, but the Depression caught up with Durant first.

Durant had overextended GM and was unsure as to how much debt he was in. Once it was determined to be about $30 million, a Du Pont-Morgan syndicate bailed him out in exchange for his resignation and his holdings in GM stock. Pierre Du Pont assumed GM's presidency, but the task of running the company fell to Alfred P. Sloan. Du Pont's influence continued at GM through the 1920s, but Sloan was made GM's president in 1923. He was very much the opposite of Durant, being detached, cool, and analytical. He began implementing his earlier plan, emphasizing structures, systems, and policies, delineating a clear chain of authority. Strict fiscal and inventory controls became a top priority.

At the same time a certain amount of decentralization and autonomy was allowed to remain. Decisions at the top became group decisions rather than individual ones. Sloan eliminated companies within GM that weren't pulling their weight. This included auto maker Scripps-Booth, whose rather stylish car had become diminished under Chevrolet/GM ownership. Chevrolet was also considered for elimination, but Sloan argued for saving it, as it was essential that GM offer a mass market car. William S. Knudsen, Henry Ford's former production manager, was brought in as Chevrolet's new president. Production rose from 130,855 in 1921 to 547,724 in 1926. By then Chevrolet offered a more stylish and better engineered car than its Ford rival.

Charles F. Kettering played an important role at this time, heading research involving both GM and DuPont. One result was a resilient, fast-drying lacquer called Duco, which significantly cut body finishing time, and was subsequently offered in a wide range of colors. Kettering also solved the industrywide problem of engine "knock" by developing tetraethyl lead. This resulted in a GM-Standard Oil of New Jersey partnership forming the Ethyl Corporation to manufacture Ethyl gasoline.

Alfred P. Sloan oversaw GM's acquisition of Britain's Vauxhall Motors in 1925 and Germany's Opel firm in 1929. He was also involved in the introduction of GM's companion cars; Oakland's (1926-2010) Pontiac, Cadillac's (1927-40) LaSalle, Oldsmobile's (1929-30) Viking, and Buick's (1930) Marquette. These were all separate brands, but marketed under the aegis of their respective companions. While the Viking and Marquette were well built, their introduction at the beginning of the Great Depression proved fatal. Pontiac became the most successful, quickly gaining popularity and outselling its parent, Oakland, by a wide margin. Oakland's last model was produced in 1931, and in 1932 Oakland Motor Car Co. became Pontiac Motor Co. Sloan introduced annual styling changes at GM, and created the concept of "planned obsolescence." His ideas about management were widely copied elsewhere. He continued as president until he assumed GM's board chairmanship in 1937. He passed away Feb. 17, 1966. For decades, GM was the world's top auto producer. However, stronger overseas competition forced it to discontinue Oldsmobile in 2004 and Pontiac in 2010.

Within a month of his 1920 departure from GM, Durant had raised $5 million from friends to start a new venture. Durant Motors, Inc. was formally established in New York on Jan. 12, 1921. Manufacturing facilities were soon arranged in Long Island City, New York. His Durant automobile, first appearing in 1921, was intended to compete at the Oakland price level. It was powered by a 4-cylinder, 35-hp overhead-valve Continental engine. The touring model was the cheapest, priced at $890. In 1922, Durant added a 6-cylinder, 70-hp model produced in Muncie, Indiana. About 55,000 Durant cars were sold that year.

Once again, Durant was thinking on a grand scale, and began acquiring companies to further his ambitions. He acquired distressed Locomobile, a luxury car firm, in 1922, intending it to compete in the Cadillac price range. That same year he introduced his low-priced 4-cylinder, 35-hp Star, which was built in Elizabeth, New Jersey. It was intended to compete against Ford and Chevrolet, and over 100,000 were built within the first year.

In purchasing the former Willys plant in Elizabeth, Durant had also acquired a prototype 6-cylinder engine then under development. A larger, revamped version of it was used to power his 65-hp Flint car, introduced in 1923. Intended to compete at the Buick price level, it was built in Long Island City and later in Flint, Michigan. Flint prices that year ranged from the $1,195 Touring Car to a $2,085 Special Sedan. Durant Motors total 1923 production reached 172,000 vehicles, putting it fourth behind Ford, GM, and Willys-Overland. Unfortunately, this was the high point for his enterprise.

Durant couldn't get out of his old patterns; making unnecessary acquisitions, paying little attention to daily operations, getting distracted by stock market speculation, and once again overextending himself. Short of capital, he sold his Flint, Michigan factory to GM in 1926. Flint car production was moved to Elizabeth, but only about 2,000 1927 models were built before production ceased. Durant sold his Long Island City facility to Ford in 1927. No Durant cars were produced that year, but three new 6-cylinder Durant models appeared in 1928, built in Elizabeth. Durant sales were 43,951 that year.

Star production was phased out beginning in 1927. Its 6-cylinder model became the Durant Model 55 in 1928. Its 4-cylinder model was discontinued in 1928, becoming the Durant Model 4-40 in 1929. Locomobile became a casualty after only a small number of 1929 cars were produced. Durant models were the firm's last chance, but in 1931 only 7,270 were sold. Production halted in 1932 and the firm was liquidated the following year. Durant himself declared bankruptcy in 1936. However, he subsequently became involved in a grocery business, a bowling alley venture, and a drive-in restaurant. He passed away in New York on Mar. 18, 1947, at age 85.

CADILLAC AND LASALLE

Cadillac's origins lie in the 1899 creation of the Detroit Automobile Co. by Henry Ford and a group of wealthy Detroit investors. The firm was reorganized as the Henry Ford Co. on Nov. 30, 1901. However, early the next year his backers turned against him because he seemed more intent on racing cars than producing them. When they brought in Henry Martyn Leland, of the Leland & Faulconer firm, to give an appraisal, Ford reacted angrily and quickly resigned. His investors were intent on dissolving the firm, but were persuaded by Leland to keep going. To convince them, he brought along a 1-cylinder 10-hp engine that he had built earlier to show Ransom E. Olds. It was an improvement over an Olds engine slated for Leland & Faulconer production, but Olds preferred to stick with his original design, leaving Leland with his prototype. It was this that convinced Ford's former backers to stay the course. Their firm was reorganized as Cadillac Automobile Co., and Leland's engine powered its first cars.

The original arrangement with Leland & Faulconer was for them to be the suppliers of engines, steering gears, and transmissions. However, while that part ran smoothly, the assembly operation at Cadillac didn't. In October 1905, Leland & Faulconer and Cadillac were merged to become Cadillac Motor Car Co., with Leland becoming general manager. Leland was a perfectionist and his background was in precision engineering. Born to a Quaker family in Barton, Vermont, on Feb. 16, 1843, he had worked at Samuel Colt's gun factory in Hartford, Connecticut, and later for Brown & Sharpe, a Rhode Island tool and machinery company. Coming to Detroit in 1890, Leland became associated with Robert C. Faulconer, a wealthy lumberman, and Charles H. Norton, a tool designer. Although specializing in precision gear manufacture, their firm engaged in other kinds of production, including both steam and gasoline engines.

Cadillac's first Model A, a runabout with detachable tonneau, was completed Oct. 17, 1902. Priced at $750, it was taken to the New York Automobile Show in January 1903, and 2,286 orders were taken. A 1-cylinder Model B was added to the lineup in 1904. For 1905, Cadillac offered the 1-cylinder Models B, C, E, and F, and the 4-cylinder Model D, the latter available only as a 5-passenger tonneau. Using a shaft drive, its 300.7 cubic inch L-head engine developed 30-hp. The 1-cylinder lettered models were serial improvements over the original Model A. Throughout this evolution, the wheelbase length gradually extended and a longer hood took shape. Runabout, tonneau, surrey, and delivery body styles were available in 1905. Cadillac's first Limousine was offered for 1906.

Having standardized and interchangeable parts was one of Leland's immediate goals and in 1908 Cadillac became the first automobile company in the world to achieve it. That year, F.S. Bennett, Cadillac's London dealer, staged an innovative test. He had three 1-cylinder Cadillac cars dismantled under Royal Automobile Club supervision at Brooklands. The parts were mixed together and then three cars re-assembled from them. All started up immediately and were then run on the Brooklands track. For this impressive demonstration of quality and precision, Cadillac won England's 1908 Dewar Trophy. It was awarded annually to the car making the greatest contribution to the advancement of the automotive industry. This achievement became the basis for Cadillac's subsequent slogan, "The Standard of the World."

Cadillac discontinued its previous 1- and 4-cylinder models in 1908, instead concentrating on a single line, the 4-cylinder, 33-hp Model 30 for 1909. By doing so it managed to offer a higher quality car at a cheaper price. The Model 30 that year was offered in touring, demi-tonneau, and roadster body styles, all priced at $1,400. Coupes and limousines were added for 1910, and Model 30 production ended in 1911.

Previously, in 1909, Cadillac had been purchased by GM for $5.5 million. William C. Durant lost control of GM to bankers in 1910. However, Cadillac's solvency and good standing helped to keep GM from a complete breakup. For 1912, a 40-hp, 4-cylinder engine was introduced, as well as an electric self-starter and electric lights developed by Delco's Charles F. Kettering. In England, three Cadillacs were lined up and tested for 1,000 startups each. They passed the test and Cadillac received a second Dewar trophy. The starting price for a new Cadillac that year was $1,800.

While Cadillac had only offered 4-cylinder engines through 1914, its status improved the following year when its only engine option was a 70-hp V-8. The company's timing must have been better than two other firms which had introduced V-8 production models in the 1906-7 period, Buffum and Hewitt. In both cases the companies quickly went out of business. Following Cadillac's lead were companies like Scripps-Booth, Abbott-Detroit, Peerless, and King who soon introduced their own V-8 models.

Cadillac Type 51 prices for 1915 ranged from $1,975 for a Touring Car or Roadster to $3,600 for a 7-passenger Berline Limousine. From then through 1923, the firm's models were designated by a sequence of odd numbers; Type 53 for 1916, Type 55 for 1917, Type 57 for 1918-19, Type 59 for 1920-21, and Type 61 for 1922-23. During this period a number of refinements were made and a wider range of body styles was offered. Among the improvements were detachable cylinder heads, first offered for 1918.

After a disagreement with GM president William C. Durant in 1917, Henry Leland and his son Wilfred left Cadillac. Succeeding Leland as general manager was Richard H. Collins, who left for Peerless in 1921. Herbert H. Rice succeeded Collins, but he was replaced in 1925 by one of the seven Fisher brothers, Lawrence P. Fisher, who held the job into the mid-1930s. There were changes in the position of chief engineer as well, but with the appointment of Ernest Seaholm around 1923, that job was filled into World War II.

For 1924-25, Cadillac introduced its V-63 model powered by a V-8 engine generating in excess of 80-hp. It featured 4-wheel brakes and an inherently balanced crankshaft. Prices that year ran from a $3,085 Touring Car, Phaeton, or Roadster to a 7-passenger Limousine or Town Brougham at $4,600. Annual sales in this period were typically over 20,000 cars.

Cadillac's Series 314, produced in 1926-27, was powered by an 85.5-hp V-8. It was advertised as "The New Ninety Degree Cadillac" because of the 90-degree mounted engine. The wheelbase was extended from 132 in. to 138 in. on some body styles. For 1927, custom bodies by coach building firms like Fleetwood, Willoughby, and Brunn were offered. GM subsequently purchased Fleetwood and made it a division within Fisher Body Co.

On Mar. 5, 1927, Cadillac introduced its companion car, the LaSalle, which subsequently was marketed through its dealerships. Intended to fill a pricing gap between Cadillac and Buick, the LaSalle was designed by Harley J. Earl, who was influenced by the styling of the Hispano-Suiza. Earl had been brought in from California, and he later oversaw all GM styling and design. The LaSalle, powered by Cadillac's 85.5-hp engine, was a more handsome and stylish car than the Cadillac, and offered a range of body styles having either 128-inch or 134-inch wheelbases. Annual sales for LaSalle peaked at 22,961 in 1929, and then went down as the Great Depression moved in. While it underwent a number of subsequent styling and design changes, it had to compete with a low-priced Packard model and its Cadillac sibling, which had the advantage in name prestige. In all, LaSalle built about 205,000 cars before it ceased production in 1940.

Cadillac's 1928-29 Series 341, designed by Harley Earl, was a real stylistic improvement over previous models. Both synchromesh transmission and safety glass were introduced for the 1929 version. For 1930, Cadillac introduced its Series 353 V-8 models and its Series 452 V-16 models. That year V-16 prices ranged from $5,350 to $9,700. For 1931, Cadillac added the Series 370-A V-12 models. Both the V-16 and V-12 engines were of the overhead-valve type, developing 165-hp and 135-hp respectively. The Cadillacs of this period were long and very elegant in appearance, having a beauty of style unique to the early 1930s. Luckily, Cadillac survived both the Great Depression and the recent 2008 bailout, and is with us today, still making some very excellent cars. Henry Leland, the man so long associated with the firm, passed away on Mar. 26, 1932, in Detroit.

THE THREE P'S

Known as the Three P's, Packard, Pierce-Arrow, and Peerless were among America's finest luxury cars, and were in close competition with each other, as well as other firms like Winton, Cadillac, Locomobile, Marmon, and Lincoln. All entered business around the turn of the century. In their day, they were all beautiful, elegantly styled, with lavish interiors and powerful motors. Later on, both Peerless and Pierce-Arrow became victims of the Great Depression, but Packard continued in business until 1958. Both Pierce-Arrow and Packard shared the dubious distinction of having been merged with Studebaker prior to their demise, and Studebaker itself halted production in 1966.

In Aug. 1898 James Ward Packard of Warren, Ohio, made a trip to Cleveland and purchased a new Winton vehicle. On his 50-mile return trip there were delays because of overheating and a broken sprocket chain. Unhappy with this, Packard returned to confront Winton, giving him some suggestions. Winton in turn retorted something like: "If you are so smart, Mr. Packard, why don't you make a car yourself." Packard decided to do just that, completing his first motor carriage in November, 1899. Helping him out were two former Winton employees, George Weiss and William A. Hatcher.

At the time, Packard and his brother, William Doud, owned the Ohio & New York Co., a manufacturer of incandescent lamps and transformers. Using the company shop, four more "Model A" carriages were built by the end of the year. A Model B followed in 1900, with 49 being built. These cars all had a 1-cylinder, 7-hp engine, chain drive, and a 2-speed planetary transmission. Early Packard innovations included the "H" slot gearshift which was later widely used in the industry. In September, 1900, this automotive endeavor became the Ohio Automobile Co. A year later the company adopted the slogan, "Ask the Man Who Owns One." Packard's 1-cylinder, 12-hp Model C, equipped with a steering wheel, followed in 1901. The 1-cylinder, 12-hp Model F of 1902 had a 3-speed sliding gear transmission. That same year the company introduced a 2-cylinder, 24-hp car, the Model G.

Henry B. Joy, a wealthy Detroit businessman, had purchased a Packard and became interested in the company. Investing heavily in it, he acquired a controlling interest. On Oct. 13, 1902, the company name was changed to Packard Motor Car Co., and a year later it was moved from Warren to Detroit. In the summer of 1903, a Packard Model F was driven by Tom Fetch from San Francisco to New York. The 61-day trip beat a record set by Winton only a month earlier. Fetch had been accompanied by Marius Krarup, editor of *The Automobile,* and this brought the company some very helpful publicity. Also in 1903, Packard's 4-cylinder, 24-hp Model K was introduced. That fall a racer version of it, the "Gray Wolf," set a speed record at Daytona of 77.6 mph. Packard's earliest vehicles were of the runabout or surrey type. The first tonneau was offered in 1902 and the first limousine in 1905.

The 4-cylinder, 22-hp Model L, introduced in 1904, was the first to have the distinctive radiator shell styling that subsequently became Packard's hallmark. The 1905 4-cylinder Model N had a 28-hp L-head engine. The 4-cylinder, 24-hp 1906 Model S was equipped with a T-head engine. The 4-cylinder, 30-hp Model 30, introduced in 1907, was produced for a number of years afterwards, as was the smaller 4-cylinder, 18-hp Model 18, which came out in 1909. The 6-cylinder, 48-hp T-head Packard "48" began production in 1912. A 38-hp, 6-cylinder L-head Packard "38" was introduced in 1913. It was the first Packard to have an electric starter and left-side steering.

In 1916, Alvan Macauley succeeded Henry Joy as company president. Joy resigned as chairman of the board the following year. Packard introduced its "Twin-Six" V-12 in 1916. Having an L-head engine, it had a top speed of 70 mph. It was the world's first 12-cylinder car to go into regular production. From then until 1921 this model was the only car the company offered. Packard had produced trucks since 1908 and built many during World War I. It was also involved in development and production of the Liberty aircraft engine.

In 1921 Packard introduced its L-head "Single-Six" model to provide a more economical alternative. "Twin-Six" production ended in 1923, with an L-head "Single-Eight" replacing it in 1924. Packard's last year for 6-cylinder models was 1928. As the decade waned, the company's eights could be had in Standard, Custom, and DeLuxe versions.

In his book, *The Automobile in America,* Stephen W. Sears gave this eloquent assessment of Packard at this time:

> Among the Olympian cars of those pre-depression years, however, Packard dominated the field by a large margin. It was the most widely owned, and the most widely desired among those striving for an automotive symbol of status and success. Over the years, under Henry Joy and then Alvan Macauley, Packard built up a strong tradition of excellence and a loyal following, and the 1920s designs were superbly executed. "The Packard of that day was a classic—aesthetically and otherwise," admitted Cadillac's long-time chief engineer, Ernest W. Seaholm, "it was our bogey for many years." The car's long hood enclosing the powerful straight-8 engine gave it proportions that were sleek and rakish yet not too radical for the carriage trade. Packard was a "gentleman's car, built by gentlemen,"and it was a gentlemanly success: in 1928 it achieved sales of fifty thousand, far and away the best of the Olympian era.

Fortunately, Packard was sufficiently strong then to weather the Great Depression which followed. James Ward Packard passed away on March 20, 1928. Henry B. Joy died on Nov. 6, 1936.

The George N. Pierce Co. of Buffalo, New York, emerged from a company founded in 1865 that made bird cages and ice boxes. Bicycles were added to its product line in 1896. The company treasurer, Col. Charles Clifton, promoted the idea of producing automobiles, and a steam vehicle was built in 1900. This effort was a failure, but the company produced a gas vehicle that November, powered by a 1-cylinder De Dion engine. Englishman David Fergusson became chief engineer in 1901 and stayed for the next 20 years.

Production of the Pierce Motorette began later that year. The original 2.75-hp version was followed by a 3.5-hp model. Total production for both reached 150 units by the end of 1902. The lineup in 1903 had a 1-cylinder, 5-hp Motorette, a 1-cylinder, 6-hp Stanhope and a 2-cylinder, 15-hp Tonneau. The latter was the first to have a front-mounted vertical engine of the Panhard type. The company introduced its "Arrow" designation in 1904. Also that year, its 4-cylinder "Great Arrow" came out. A Pierce Great Arrow was entered in the first Glidden Tour in 1905 and won it.

The competition included Packard, Peerless, Locomobile, Cadillac, and a number of luxury European cars. This victory was followed by four more in successive years. The company added a 6-cylinder model in 1907, the Great Arrow 65 (Later the Model 66). Pierce dropped the Great Arrow name at the end of the 1908 model year. In 1909, the company name was changed to Pierce-Arrow Motor Car Co. For a number of years after, it offered the 6-cylinder Models 38, 48, and 66; these numbers indicating the amount of horsepower. In 1911, the company began building trucks. This became very lucrative during World War I and truck production continued to 1932.

Fender-mounted headlamps, introduced in 1913, became Pierce-Arrow's most distinctive feature. By early 1915, total company production had reached 12,000 automobiles. In October 1918, the Dual-Valve Six engine was introduced. Following this the company went through an unstable period of leadership after its old management retired. But after Charles L. Sheppy took over as chief engineer and Myron E. Forbes became president in 1921, things normalized. Pierce-Arrow was one of the last firms to convert from right-side steering to left-side, only doing so in 1920.

The Series 80 models, having an L-head 6-cylinder, 70-hp engine, were added to the company's lineup in 1924. Four-wheel brakes with a vacuum-powered booster became standard in 1926. However Pierce-Arrow needed to make stronger changes. In clinging to its 6-cylinder tradition, the firm slowly fell behind its competitors, most of whom were now selling higher powered 8- and 12-cylinder models. Some also thought Pierce-Arrow's styling had become dated.

In 1928 a merger of the company was arranged with Studebaker. The following year Pierce-Arrow introduced a 125-hp, straight-8 engine and sold 10,000 cars. Afterwards, other styling and engineering changes were made, including adding a 140-hp V-12 model in 1931. The firm exhibited its streamlined "Silver Arrow" dream car in 1933, but it never went into production. In 1932, during the depth of the Great Depression, Studebaker and Cleveland's White Motor Co. attempted a merger. However the merger was eventually blocked by some disgruntled White stockholders. Studebaker's money ran out and in March

1933 it was forced into receivership. Pierce-Arrow was sold off to investors with White taking over its truck division. This setback proved too much for longtime Studebaker president Albert R. Erskine, who on June 30 of that year shot himself in the heart. Pierce-Arrow's sales continued downwards, and in 1938 it expired.

The Peerless Manufacturing Co. of Cleveland, Ohio, began with clothes wringers, proceeded to other products including bicycles, and in 1900 decided to make automobiles. The initial offering was the Motorette buggy, powered by a 1-cylinder De Dion engine. Louis P. Mooers, who had built a gas-powered vehicle in 1897, was hired to be chief engineer and he completed his first prototype, a 1-cylinder vehicle in 1901. A 2-cylinder car with vertically-mounted engine came next. In 1902, the firm built 90 vehicles and changed its name to Peerless Motor Car Co. By then, it had gotten into racing, with Mooers driving much of the time. In 1904, he designed the 60-hp Peerless "Green Dragon" and hired the famous driver Barney Oldfield to race it. Breaking many speed records, it provided Peerless with valuable publicity and nationwide name recognition.

At the New York Automobile Show of January 1904, Peerless introduced a 4-cylinder car, very modern in design for the time. Featuring a forward-tilting steering wheel, it came in side-entrance tonneau and limousine models. In 1905, Charles B. Schmidt, previously with Packard, was hired to replace Mooers. Schmidt took the company out of racing and concentrated on the luxury car market. "All that the Name Implies," became the new company slogan. Company production for 1906 totaled 1,176 cars, and in 1907 Peerless introduced a 6-cylinder, 50-hp model. Unfortunately, from 1913 through World War I, Peerless went through a number of managerial changes, but despite these disruptions, managed to bring out a V-8 model in 1916, shortly after Cadillac had introduced its own.

Richard H. Collins, a former president and general manager of Cadillac, took over the firm in 1921, bringing with him some Cadillac engineers. At this time, Peerless' V-8 engine came in 33.8 and 80 horsepower versions. Despite the economic downturn, the company did relatively well in the early 1920s, with annual production figures ranging from 3,500 to 6,000 vehicles. Unfortunately, management changes continued and Collins was forced out at the end of 1923.

This lack of stability in the organization remained a problem at Peerless until its end in 1931. Not helping matters was the company's reputation for overly conservative styling. The 1930 lineup, designed by Russian emigre Alexis de Sakhnoffsky, brought a welcome change. However, the Great Depression had arrived and it was too little, too late. The last and finest Peerless was a V-16 prototype, with body by Murphy. Unfortunately, it never went into production.

MAXWELL, CHRYSLER, AND DODGE BROTHERS

Jonathan Dixon Maxwell was an engineer who had gained experience at both the Olds and Northern auto firms. He formed a partnership in 1903 with Benjamin Briscoe, a Detroit sheet metal manufacturer. Briscoe, it may be remembered, had previously bankrolled

Buick, but had pulled out after losing confidence in the firm. Thus was formed the Maxwell-Briscoe Motor Co., which gained additional financing from banker J.P. Morgan.

The first car built at the firm's Tarrytown, New York, factory in 1904 was a 2-cylinder, 8 to 12-hp, 2-passenger Tourabout. Among its features was right-side steering, honeycomb radiator, 2-speed planetary transmission, and shaft drive. First offered as the 1905 Model L, it sold for $750. A companion vehicle that year was the 2-cylinder, 16-hp Model H Touring Car, priced at $1,400. These cars were well designed, well built, and quickly gained popularity. Production for the 1905 model year totaled 823, giving Maxwell eighth place in the industry. For the firm's 1906 lineup other models were introduced. This included the 4-cylinder 36 to 40-hp Model M, offered as a 5-passenger Touring Car for $3,000.

During the 1905-06 period, the firm acquired additional production facilities in Chicago and Pawtucket, Rhode Island. Maxwell built 2,161 cars in 1906, moving to fifth in industry rankings. It also won the Deming Trophy in the 1906 Glidden Tour. From 1906 through 1912, Maxwell offered both 2- and 4-cylinder models, introducing a 3-speed sliding gear transmission in 1907. During this time it was involved in light car racing and other competitions, and under sales manager Cadwallader Washburn Kelsey, was vigorously promoted in other sensational and innovative ways.

Benjamin Briscoe had ambitions of creating an automotive empire. His first effort in 1907 involved teaming up with William C. Durant to acquire Ford and Reo, but this didn't work out. In 1910, along with his brother Frank, he started United States Motor Co., combining the solid Maxwell enterprise with a number of more troubled firms. This group included Columbia, Brush, Stoddard-Dayton, Courier (a Stoddard-Dayton subsidiary), and Alden Sampson Trucks.

Disagreeing with Briscoe's risky expansionism, Kelsey departed. Jonathan Maxwell was unhappy as well, but remained, taking over as president of Maxwell-Briscoe. Unfortunately, in 1912 United States Motor Co. collapsed and went into receivership. Walter E. Flanders, a partner in the late E-M-F auto firm and cost-cutting expert, arrived to sort out the pieces. Briscoe retreated to France, but later returned to establish Briscoe Motor Corporation at Jackson, Michigan, in 1914.

After a selloff of various assets, Maxwell was the only surviving company. Although losing its Tarrytown works and other facilities, it still retained a large factory in New Castle, Indiana. Flanders and Jonathan Maxwell reorganized the firm as Maxwell Motor Co. and relocated its headquarters to Detroit. From 1913 onwards the company built 4-cylinder models, but in 1913-14 offered a 6-cylinder car. The company continued to be among America's top auto producers, ranking fifth with 18,000 cars in 1914, fourth in 1915 with 44,000 cars, sixth in 1916 with 69,000 cars, and sixth in 1917 with 75,000 cars.

An occasion for celebration that year was the production of Maxwell's 100,000th car. Unfortunately in 1918 the company built only 34,000 cars, but still ranked sixth in the industry. However by 1920, after the post-war recession hit, Maxwell was in real trouble. Its car had gained a bad reputation for engineering problems and its dealers were overstocked. At one point the firm had a backed-up inventory of 26,000 unsold cars, of which perhaps 16,000 sat on rail sidings. During this same period it conducted negotiations with the ailing but more prestigious Chalmers firm, and in 1922 took it over. Unfortunately this didn't help matters.

Walter Percy Chrysler was born on Apr. 2, 1875 in Wamego, Kansas. From doing farm work and other types of simple jobs, he moved on to railroad employment, starting as a roundhouse sweeper for the Union Pacific. Years later, after relocating a number of times, he was managing the American Locomotive Co. manufacturing plant in Pittsburgh. In 1910 he was recruited by Buick as works manager and moved to Flint, Michigan. In 1912 Chrysler became president of Buick and held that position until he had a falling out with GM president William C. Durant in early 1920. Upon leaving he was paid about $10 million for his GM stock.

After his departure, Chrysler was persuaded by the Chase National Bank to manage the ailing Willys-Overland firm which was in receivership. In 1908, John North Willys had taken over the distressed Overland company, based in Indianapolis. After reorganizing it, he moved the operation to Toledo. Willys' company had done very well for some years but was overextended when the postwar recession hit, at which point the bankers took over. Chrysler's job was to cut away all the fat, which among other things meant firing a lot of people.

At this time Willys-Overland was offering two lines, the 4-cylinder Overland and the 4-cylinder sleeve-valve Willys-Knight. In the works, at a former Duesenberg factory in Elizabeth, New Jersey, was a 6-cylinder prototype engine intended to power a new Willys car. Working on this project were Fred Zeder, Owen Skelton, and Carl Breer, engineers who previously had worked for Studebaker. Chrysler was very interested in this design, but when the Willys-Overland assets were auctioned off, William C. Durant outbid him for both the engine and the Elizabeth factory. Durant went on to build his Star automobile there, and the engine, enlarged and substantially modified, became the motor for the Flint car introduced in 1923. Chrysler did a good job reviving Willys-Overland; its stock rose in value, and subsequently by deft means John North Willys regained control of his firm.

During his time at Willys, Chrysler had also been consulted by his banker friends regarding the distressed Maxwell-Chalmers firm. In August 1920 he began serving as chairman of a reorganization committee. After leaving Willys-Overland in 1922, he was induced by a generous stock option and profit sharing offers to take over Maxwell-Chalmers. He brought with him Skelton, Zeder, and Breer, who later became known as the "three musketeers." They were immediately put to work assessing Maxwell's problematic 4-cylinder Model 25, the only car it had produced since 1915. This resulted in an upgraded version, subsequently advertised as "The Good Maxwell." At the same time they headed a team making further refinements on Willys' original 6-cylinder engine design, which became the first Chrysler motor.

In January 1924, Chrysler's 6-cylinder, 68-hp Model B-70 was introduced at New York's Commodore Hotel. Prices began at $1,335 and within a year 32,000 had been sold, breaking a first-year industry sales record. It was the first high-compression car offered in the medium-price field, and would operate comfortably at speeds up to 70 mph. Ralph De Palma broke stock car records with it and it performed well at Le Mans.

Maxwell was reorganized in 1925 as the Chrysler Corporation, and production of the Maxwell car was terminated. The firm's co-founder, Jonathan Maxwell, passed away on Mar. 8, 1928 in Tarrytown, New York. His former partner, Benjamin Briscoe, died on June, 26, 1945 in Dunnellon, Florida. The Maxwell automobile continued to live on in the American imagination for many years, thanks to comedian Jack Benny. Decades later, he played a wealthy tightwad who, owning a 1916 Maxwell, wouldn't spend money to buy anything newer.

A Maxwell engine was revamped for Chrysler's 4-cylinder, 38-hp Model F-58, offered in 1926. That year Chrysler also offered its 6-cylinder, 68-hp Model G-70 and the 6-cylinder, 92-hp Imperial Model E-80. Among the distinguishing features of the latter were longer wheelbases, bullet shaped headlights, and a scalloped hood and radiator design. 1926 Chrysler prices began at $890 for its Model F-58 roadster and ran to $3,695 for its standard E-80 Berline Limousine. However, more expensive custom models could be ordered. Chrysler built 135,520 cars that year, ranking it seventh in the industry. The firm maintained the same position in 1927, producing 182,195 vehicles.

In 1928 Chrysler purchased the Dodge Brothers firm for $170 million. This company had its roots in the Detroit machine shop established by John and Horace Dodge in 1901. Soon they were providing Ransom E. Olds with engines and transmissions, and afterwards had a similar arrangement with Henry Ford. They also became investors in Ford Motor Co., acquiring a 10 percent interest in the firm. By the early teens it became apparent that Ford intended to pull all of its production in-house, and was hard at work on its massive River Rouge factory, which was completed in 1914. Aware of all this, the Dodges announced in 1913 that they would stop making Ford parts and go into the car business themselves.

Their first automobile, America's first mass-produced car with a totally welded, all-steel body, was completed on Nov. 14, 1914. It was a very sturdy vehicle, having a 3-speed selective transmission, 12-volt electrical system, and a 4-cylinder, 35-hp L-head engine. Offered at $785 for both roadster and touring models, it gained instant popularity. Dodge ranked third in 1915 auto production, building about 45,000 cars. That year Ford, unhappy with the Dodge competition, part of which was financed by his stock dividends, refused to pay stockholder dividends. The brothers sued Ford, collecting back dividends, and finally in 1919 divested themselves of their stock for $25 million.

In 1916, Dodge Brothers production was 71,400 cars, ranking it fourth in the industry. That year General John J. "Black Jack" Pershing used Dodge Brothers cars in Mexico, while attempting to capture famous rebel leader Pancho Villa. During World War I, the company produced many staff cars and ambulances for the military effort overseas. In 1919, an all-steel sedan was added to the firm's lineup.

In 1920, both Dodge brothers passed away, John from pneumonia in January, and Horace from liver cirrhosis in December. Their widows selected Frederick Haynes, a long-time employee, to take over the helm. The investment firm of Dillon, Read & Co. purchased Dodge Brothers in 1925, bringing in E.G. Wilmer as president. The company's car had changed little in the intervening years and its market position was eroding. Thus in 1927, the Senior 6-cylinder series was introduced, and when the Victory and Standard models were added for 1928, the lineup became all 6-cylinder.

Chrysler's 1928 acquisition of Dodge Brothers gave him control of some excellent production facilities and a large dealer network. This provided a solid platform for entering the high-volume low-priced market. He wasted no time in doing so, introducing his 4-cylinder Plymouth Model Q on July 7 that year. It was driven into New York's Madison Square Garden arena by famed aviatrix Amelia Earhart.

Intended to compete against Ford and Chevrolet, this car was a redesign of Chrysler's 4-cylinder Model 52, which was subsequently dropped. Its 45-hp motor was a further refinement of the engine Chrysler had inherited from Maxwell. The Plymouth was offered in Roadster, Coupe, Sedan, and Touring models priced from $670 to $725. Nearly 60,000 cars were sold in the first model year. Among its features were a thin-profile radiator and 4-wheel hydraulic brakes. The Plymouth was initially sold only in Chrysler dealerships, but beginning in 1930 dealers of all Chrysler divisions carried it.

On Aug. 4, 1928, Chrysler introduced his 6-cylinder, 55-hp DeSoto for the 1929 model year. Priced from $845 to $955, the car was an instant hit and 81,065 cars were sold in the first year. This set an initial-year sales record that lasted until 1960. Before the Dodge Brothers acquisition, it had been planned for DeSoto to compete in the low-priced 6-cylinder field. Thus for a time the two companies competed head-to-head. About 1930, Dodge quietly dropped the "brothers" part of its name. That same year a 75-hp, straight-8 was added to its lineup and a 70-hp, straight-8 was added to DeSoto's. DeSoto's position in Chrysler's heirarchy was finally clarified in 1933 when it was promoted to fill the gap between Chrysler and Dodge, with Plymouth having the bottom rung.

1929 DeSoto

In 1929, Chrysler models became longer and lower, and a thin-profile radiator was added. The company also offered limited series custom models by coach builders Locke, LeBaron, and Dietrich. While Chrysler had stayed with sixes through 1930, it too added a straight-8 engine for its 1931 lineup, this one generating 100-hp. Like its competitors, Chrysler Corporation had a tough time during the Great Depression, but unlike many it was a survivor. In 1933, it overtook Ford and Lincoln in overall sales, maintaining the industry's number two position until 1950.

Chrysler's revolutionary Airflow designs, built from 1934 to 1936, were ahead of their time, but unfortunately didn't receive public acceptance. In order to stay competitive Chrysler had to drop DeSoto in 1961 and Plymouth in 2001. Thanks to help from Lee Iacocco, the 1979 U.S. Congress, Bob Lutz, President Obama, and Fiat, we still have Chrysler and Dodge with us today. Walter P. Chrysler passed away on Aug. 18, 1940 in Kings Point, New York.

MERCER AND STUTZ

Mercer became famous for its Raceabout model, one of America's first legendary sports cars. Mercer Automobile Company was founded in May 1909 at Trenton, in Mercer County, New Jersey. Money was put up by the Roebling and Kuser families, both of whom had been involved in construction of the Brooklyn Bridge, which was completed in 1883. Mercer rose from the ashes of the Walter and short-lived Roebling-Planche cars which had been built in Trenton's old Consumers Brewery. The 1910 Mercer was powered by a 4-cylinder, L-head Beaver engine and was offered in touring, speedster, and toy-tonneau models.

The T-head Raceabout, offered for the 1911 model year, was the brainchild of Washington A. Roebling II, the son of Charles G. Roebling. Finley R. Porter was the engineer in charge of the project. Painted yellow and built relatively low to the ground, the Raceabout was powered by a 300 cubic inch, 4-cylinder, 34-hp engine. Having a 116 inch wheelbase, it was spare and lean, with fenders, hood, monocle windshield, two bucket seats, a cylindrical gas tank, and rear-mounted spare tire. These were very fast cars for their day, winning five of six major races entered that year. While the original model had a 3-speed gearbox, a 4-speed transmission became optional in 1912. While driving a Raceabout at the Los Angeles Speedway that year, Brian DePalma managed to set eight new class world records. Barney Oldfield drove Raceabouts for a time, and a serious competition developed between Mercer and Stutz.

1917 Stutz Racer

Unfortunately, Washington A. Roebling II was lost in the April 1912 sinking of the Titanic. Finley Porter left the firm in 1914 and was replaced by Eric H. Delling, who quit in 1916. For Mercer's 1915 models, Delling replaced the T-head engine with a 4-cylinder 70-hp L-head motor. He changed the Raceabout by adding bench seats and a full-length windshield. In 1917 Ferdinand W. Roebling passed away, followed by Charles G. Roebling in 1918. The deaths of these important family members left Mercer in a distressed state. It was taken over in October 1919 by a Wall Street group and reorganized as Mercer Motors Co. Emlen S. Hare, a former Packard vice-president, was put in charge. By December his Hare's Motors Inc. had acquired a substantial part of Locomobile, and in January 1920 took over Simplex.

Up to this time Mercer's output had been quite limited. Its 1920, prices ranged from the $4,400 Raceabout to the $5,750 Limousine. Hare wanted to increase Mercer production to 50,000 cars per year, but his venture collapsed in August 1921. Mercer control reverted to some of its previous insiders. Raceabout production ended in 1922, and Mercer fell into receivership, only producing small numbers of cars before closing in 1925. Oddly, Harry M. Wahl, a former Durant associate, formed Mercer Motors Corporation in November 1929, in a futile attempt to revive the firm. Powered by a 140-hp, straight-8 Continental engine, his new automobile was intended to be offered in five models. However, only one car was actually built. It was shown at the New York Automobile Show in January 1931, and then Mercer quietly faded away.

The Stutz Bearcat was the most legendary sports car of its time. Its original builder, Harry C. Stutz, grew up on an Ohio farm, and showed an early interest in machinery. In 1903, at age 27, he moved to Indianapolis and soon became involved in automotive work. His employers included American Motors Co., builder of the American Underslung, and Marion Motor Car Co. While at Marion he met Gil Anderson, who afterwards became his star racing driver.

In 1909 the Indianapolis Speedway was shut down so that it could be paved with brick. While a number of races were scheduled for 1910, it was decided that beginning in 1911 only a single spectacular event, a 500-mile race, would be held each year. When this plan was publicized, Stutz quit Marion and in 1910 set up Stutz Auto Parts Co. Although his new firm specialized in transmission and axle production, Stutz wanted to become a car manufacturer. Seeing racing as a way to get in, he devoted part of his time to building a racer, completing it just before the 1911 event. It had a Wisconsin 4-cylinder, 50-hp T-head engine, and a special compact differential/gearbox combination of his own design.

By this time Stutz had gathered financial backing and was tooling up for car production. The May 30, 1911 race attracted wide attention and drew 40 entries. Stutz's automobile, driven by Gil Anderson, placed 11th in the race. Although not among the top contenders, it drew praise in Indianapolis for maintaining an average speed of 68 mph, and requiring no pit stops for repairs. This solid performance inspired Stutz's new company slogan; "The Car That Made Good in a Day." Winning that first Indianapolis 500 race was Ray Harroun, in the Marmon "Wasp," averaging 74.59 mph. In his car he mounted a mirror so that he could see the track behind. This is the first known use of an automobile rear-view mirror.

Ideal Motor Car Co. was set up to manufacture Stutz's new cars. Mechanically identical to his racer, these were offered in roadster, toy-tonneau, and touring models, all priced at $2,000. At this time Stutz was personally overseeing construction of each car. In 1912 his 120-inch wheelbase Bearcat model was introduced. Like its Mercer Raceabout counterpart it was low and lean. Among its features were a monocle windshield, bucket seats, cylindrical gas tank, trunk, and rear-mounted spare tire. Stutz also offered a 6-cylinder, 60-hp engine option for its 1912 models, these coming with a 124-inch wheelbase.

The company was very involved in racing that year, winning some important events. Racing on the West Coast was Earl Cooper, who although driving a Stutz, operated independent of company sanction until 1915. In 1913 Ideal and Stutz Auto Parts were merged to become Stutz Motor Car Co. That year its "White Squadron" captured eight of ten premier racing events, and Earl Cooper became national driving champion. The 1915 competition was similarly good for Stutz. Its racers were powered that year by a Wisconsin built 16-valve, single-overhead-camshaft engine. In 1915, additional publicity came when Cannon Ball Baker drove a Stutz Bearcat from San Diego to New York in 11 days, 7 hours, and 15 minutes, breaking the transcontinental record.

While having previously acquired engines from suppliers, Stutz opted to produce its own 80-hp, 16-valve, 4-cylinder T-head for 1917. Its original factory had been set up to build 500 cars annually. However production had increased from 266 cars in 1912 to 1,535 in 1916. Factory expansion this time required Stutz to go public. Unfortunately, Wall Street speculator, Allan A. Ryan, managed to acquire a controlling interest of the firm. In 1919 Harry Stutz sold his stock and left to build a new car called the H.C.S.

Ryan was a clever manipulator, and in 1920 attempted a stock market corner which became a national scandal. Stutz prices jumped from $100 to $391 per share in the space of two months. However, Ryan's maneuver threatened to bankrupt some important people on New York's Stock Exchange board. Thus aroused, these powerful adversaries ultimately had him ejected from his seat there, which led to his bankruptcy. In 1922 Ryan's holdings were auctioned off, and Charles M. Schwab of Bethlehem Steel acquired Stutz at $20 per share.

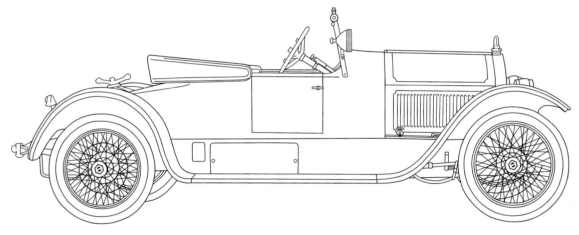

1921 Stutz Roadster

The company was in difficult circumstances at this time. For 1923 it introduced its Special Six models powered by a 6-cylinder, 70-hp, overhead-valve engine. However sales were disappointing, and Bearcat production ended with the 1924 model. In a 1925 reorganization Frederic Ewan Moscovics became Stutz president and he brought in Belgian designer Paul Bastien. This change brought a renaissance to the firm. Company emphasis shifted from performance to safety, beauty, and comfort, attracting a new upscale clientele, however the old Stutz was not dead.

For 1926 a 92-hp Vertical Eight engine was introduced. It had a single-overhead-camshaft with 16 valves, powered by a Link Belt chain drive. The new cars were beautifully styled, built lower to the ground, and could reach speeds of 75 mph. In the automotive world they became a sensation and in 1926 Stutz production hit a record 5,000 cars. For the first time in its history, Stutz became a luxury car. Some models were given chic French names, and custom bodies were offered by coach building firms like Weymann and Le Baron. Prices rose from $2,995, the same for all 1926 models, to $6,985 for a Transformable Cabriolet in 1930.

Introduced in 1927 was Stutz's elegantly designed 2-passenger Black Hawk Speedster, priced at $4,895. It was equipped with a high-compression head, increasing horsepower to 125. Many of these had boattail styling. Stutz revived its racing program that year, entering the Black Hawk in stock car competition. It won every major event in which it competed, and in 1928 placed second at the Le Mans Grand Prix.

Unfortunately Stutz's good years didn't last. On April 25, 1928, Stutz driver Frank Lockhart was killed while attempting to break the land speed record at Daytona. This brought Stutz's racing program to a halt. Production had begun to fall in 1927, and Moskovics left in early 1929. Then the Great Depression hit. However, Schwab raised more money, allowing Stutz to bring out its DV-32 model in 1931. This car had a 156-hp, straight-8 engine, designed by Fred Duesenberg. Among its features was a cylinder head with twin overhead-camshafts and 4 valves per cylinder.

The Bearcat model was revived for that year, and a Super Bearcat of shorter wheelbase was also offered. Both cars were guaranteed to go over 100 mph. Unfortunately, they were extravagant anachronisms in a sober new age of deep anxiety and pessimism. Production declined precipitously to six cars in 1934, and terminated in January 1935. The Stutz firm declared bankruptcy in 1938 and was liquidated the following year. The company's founder, Harry C. Stutz, passed away on June 26, 1930, and is buried in Indianapolis.

AUBURN, DUESENBERG AND CORD

The Auburn automobile had its origins in the Eckhart Carriage Co., founded by Charles Eckhart at Auburn, Indiana in 1874. His sons, Frank and Morris, took over the firm in 1893. In 1900 they built a one-cylinder gas vehicle with chain-drive and tiller steering, and with $2,500 of capital started Auburn Automobile Co. The company's first two years involved as much experimentation as production. By 1905 their cars had been built in runabout, tonneau, and touring models. That year Auburn introduced its first 2-cylinder car. Its first four came in 1909, and its first six in 1912. For most of this period Auburn cars sold in the $1,250-1,650 price range, but the 6-cylinder models were priced higher.

Controlling interest of the firm was acquired in 1919 by a Chicago investor group that included William Wrigley, Jr. That same year the Auburn Beauty-SIX was introduced. While it was a more attractive car than any previous Auburn, it arrived as the postwar recession was beginning. Only 15,717 cars were sold in the next four years. In 1924 Errett Lobban Cord, a young and innovative business genius, became general manager of Auburn. He took the job for no pay, but with the option of buying controlling interest if he could turn things around. Within a short time he disposed of 700 unsold cars, using nickel plating and attractive repainting to cosmetically enhance their appearance.

In 1925 the Auburn Model 8-88 was introduced. It was powered by an 8-cylinder Lycoming engine successfully mounted on the old 6-cylinder chassis. The original version had a 65-hp engine, but an 88-hp option became available in 1926. That year Auburn introduced a very attractive styling arrangement involving three-tone paint combinations and a symmetrical beltline, Starting from behind the radiator cap, two lines swept diagonally backwards over the curve of each side of the hood, and then straight back around the sides to meet in the rear. Cord was successful in turning Auburn around, and in 1926 he became company president.

In 1927, Auburn decided to challenge Stutz in stock car racing. For 1928, it introduced its Model 8-115 powered by a 115-hp, straight-8 engine. Having 4-wheel hydraulic brakes and Bijur lubrication, it was very attractively priced, ranging from the $1,995 Roadster to the $2,395 Phaeton. Among model options was the Boattail Speedster priced at $2,195. One of these was driven that year at Daytona by Wade Morton, reaching a speed of 108.46 mph over a measured mile. In a 24-hour endurance test at Atlantic City, an Auburn covered 2,033 miles, averaging 84.7 mph.

In 1929, a Model 8-120 was offered, and in 1930, a Model 8-125. By this time Auburn had become a very successful company and had acquired many dealers who had given up on other brand franchises. Although the Great Depression initially cut sales, Auburn had an amazingly good year in 1931 as profits matched those of 1929, and the company reached a 13th ranking in U.S. auto sales. That year Auburn was only offering the Model 8-98 with prices ranging from a $945 Brougham to a $1,395 Sedan.

In 1932, the company introduced its Model 12-160, powered by a Lycoming V-12 engine. Unfortunately, sales declined and so a 6-cylinder model was added for the 1934 lineup. By this time E.L. Cord was overextended, being involved not only with his auto interests—Auburn, Cord, Duesenberg, and Checker Cab—but a business empire that included ship-building, aviation, and part of a railroad. Auburn's last great car was the Supercharged Model 851 Speedster, introduced in 1934. Driven by Ab Jenkins at Bonneville, it maintained an average speed over 100 mph for twelve hours. However, the resultant publicity failed to generate the sales Auburn hoped for, and its 1936 models were its last.

In 1913 Fred Duesenberg, a former bicycle builder, and his brother Augie, formed the Duesenberg Motor Co. in St. Paul, Minnesota. Previously they had built 4-cylinder engines for cars raced by the Mason (later Mason-Maytag) company. The Duesenbergs continued production of their "walking beam" engine, which had horizontal-valve-rocker-arms. Used in competition cars, these were driven by famous drivers like Eddie Rickenbacker, Ralph Mulford, and Eddie O'Donnell. When America became involved in World War I automobile racing was largely suspended, and the Duesenbergs became involved in the war effort.

While the brothers were excellent engineers, they preferred to leave the business end to others. In 1916 a group of New York investors formed Duesenberg Motors Corporation and installed them in a large factory in Elizabeth, New Jersey. They produced marine engines during this period as well as some V-12 and V-16 aircraft motors. Their V-16 engine was based on Ettore Bugatti's U-16 aircraft motor built in France. However, the Duesenberg version was called the King-Bugatti because it incorporated some design changes made by U.S. Army Col. Charles Brady King. Once the war was over the brothers wanted to start working on 8-cylinder engines, but their backers weren't interested. Thus the Duesenberg factory in Elizabeth was sold off to Willys, and rights to the Duesenberg 4-cylinder engine were acquired by Rochester Motors Co. Inc.

The brothers relocated to Newark where they began building a single-overhead-camshaft straight-8 racing engine. After finding new backers, Duesenberg Automobile &

Motors Corporation was established in Indianapolis in 1920, with Newton E. Van Zandt as president. The firm's first automobile, the 1921 Model A, had the new straight-8 engine and was the first production car in America to have 4-wheel hydraulic brakes. Very fast and advanced for its time, with prices beginning at $6,500, the Model A was enthusiastically received at its debut. However, lengthy production delays and poor management practices resulted in poor sales—about 650 in six years. The company was reorganized as Duesenberg Motors Co. in 1925, with Fred Duesenberg as president, but things didn't improve much. However, all during this period Duesenberg racers did extremely well at the track, the most impressive performances being Jimmy Murphy's 1921 triumph at the Le Mans Grand Prix, and Indianapolis 500 wins in 1924, 1925, and 1927.

In 1926 E.L. Cord purchased the company, renaming it Duesenberg, Inc. Fred Duesenberg was instructed to build the best car he possibly could. In the meantime, for 1927, the Model X, an improved version of the Model A, was introduced. Apparently only 13 were built. Duesenberg's famous Model J made its sensational debut at the New York Automobile Show on Dec. 1, 1928. Majestic in appearance, it was large and beautiful; powered by a 265-hp, straight-8 engine with twin-overhead-camshafts and four valves per cylinder. Built low to the ground, it was offered in 142.5-inch and 153.5-inch wheelbase sizes, and the chassis price was $8,500. The Model J could reach speeds of 112 to 116 mph. While Duesenberg offered bodies built in-house by Gordon Buehrig, many others were supplied by American and European coach builders.

Although this car became an international favorite of the rich and famous, it wasn't immune to the effects of the Great Depression. Production totaled only 360 cars at the end of 1931. In the meantime Fred Duesenberg designed a centrifigal supercharger, which increased horsepower to 320. Offered as an option to the Model J, the supercharged Duesenberg SJ was introduced in May 1932, with some 36 being built by October 1935. Only two Model SSJs were produced. These were built on a shorter 125-inch wheelbase for actors Gary Cooper and Clark Gable. Chrome-plated external side exhaust pipes were standard on the Model SJ, and it could reach speeds up to 135 mph. Unfortunately, on July 26, 1932, Fred Duesenberg died from complications following an accident while driving an SJ. In all, approximately 470 Model J and SJ Duesenbergs were built. Production for Duesenberg, the finest American car of its time, ended in 1936.

Considered one of the most beautiful and elegant cars of its period was the Cord L-29, which made its debut in August 1929. It was built by Auburn Automobile Co. in Auburn and Connersville, Indiana. E.L. Cord, for whom the car was named, wanted an innovative vehicle to fill the niche between his popular Auburn and the regal Duesenberg. Involved in this project were race car engineers Cornelius Van Ranst, Harry Miller, and Indy driver Leon Duray. Van Ranst, along with Tommy Milton, had built a front-wheel drive racer in 1927 that ran in the Indianapolis 500.

Front-wheel drive became the most distinctive feature of the new Cord, giving it a very low profile. It became the first US production car to have it, beating Ruxton by a few months. Another engineering innovation was X-frame bracing designed by engineer Herb Snow. The L-29 was powered by a straight-8, 125-hp Lycoming engine, and had a 137.5-inch wheelbase. Coach builders in both the US and Europe created some wonderful bodies for this car. Cord's standard Sedan was priced at $3,095 and its Phaeton and Cabriolet models at $3,295. However, as the depression deepened, prices were dropped in 1931 to $2,395 and $2,595 respectively. As sales continued to decline, L-29 production was halted on December 31, 1931.

Cord was revived for 1936 with its new front-wheel drive Model 810, powered by a 125-hp Lycoming straight-8 engine. Designed by Gordon Buehrig, it featured a distinctive "coffin nose" style front end, with a louvered wrap-around grille and disappearing headlights. Although a sensation at New York's November 1935 car show, the 810 wasn't quite ready, as it had been rushed into production at the last moment. Problems with the semi-automatic transmission slowed production, which in turn delayed delivery of new car orders for months. Owners reported other mechanical faults, all of this creating negative publicity.

The 1937 Cord Model 812 was little changed from the 810, except that a 170-hp supercharged version became optional. These cars were easily identified by their chrome-plated external side exhaust pipes. Output of both models totaled less than 3,000, when on Aug. 7, 1937 production halted for good. During this time E.L. Cord had been battling both the Bureau of Internal Revenue and the Securities & Exchange Commission. He ended up selling off his holdings, and the new owners decided against further automobile production. Mr. Cord later became wealthy from media and real estate investments. He passed away in Reno, Nevada on January 2, 1974.

HONORABLE MENTION

Adams-Farwell (Dubuque 1905-13), ALCO (Providence 1909-13), American Underslung (Indianapolis 1906-14), Apperson (Kokomo 1902-26), Chalmers (Detroit 1908-23), Chandler (Cleveland 1913-29), Cole (Indianapolis 1909-25), Cunningham (Rochester 1907-36), Dort (Flint 1915-24), Du Pont (Wilmington, Delaware 1919-31), Essex (Detroit 1919-32), Franklin (Syracuse 1902-34), Gardner (St. Louis 1920-31), Graham-Paige & Graham (Dearborn 1928-41), Haynes-Apperson & Haynes (Kokomo, 1898-1925), Hudson (Detroit 1910-54), Hupmobile (Detroit 1909-41), Jewett (Detroit 1922-27), Jordan (Cleveland 1917-31), King (Detroit & Buffalo 1911-24), Kissel Kar & Kissel (Hartford, Wisconsin 1907-31), Lambert (Anderson, Indiana 1906-17), Locomobile (Bridgeport, Connecticut 1900-29), Lozier (Plattsburgh & Detroit 1905-18), Marmon (Indianapolis 1902-33), McFarlan (Connersville, Indiana 1910-28), Metz (Waltham 1909-21), Mitchell (Racine 1903-23), Moon (St. Louis 1905-29), Nash (Kenosha 1917-54), National (Indianapolis 1900-24), Overland (Terre-Haute, Indianapolis, & Toledo 1903-26), Owen Magnetic (New York, Cleveland, & Wilkes Barre 1915-20), Paige-Detroit & Paige (Detroit 1910-27). Premier (Indianapolis 1902-25), Roamer (Streator, Illinois & Kalamazoo 1916-29), Ruxton (St. Louis & Hartford, Wisconin 1929-30), Pungs-Finch (Detroit 1904-10), Scripps-Booth (Detroit 1912-22), Simplex (New York & New Brunswick, New Jersey 1907-19), Stearns & Stearns-Knight (Cleveland 1901-29), Studebaker (South Bend 1902-58), Templar (Cleveland 1917-24), Thomas (Buffalo 1903-18), Velie (Moline 1909-29), Whippet (Toledo 1927-31), White (Cleveland 1900-18), Wills Sainte Claire (Marysville, Michigan 1921-27), Willys-Knight (Toledo 1914-33), Winton (Cleveland 1896-1924).

PLATE 1

Top Left: Dr. Church's Steam Carriage, England, 1832.

Top Right: C.1900 Gardner-Serpollet Steam Runabout, Paris. Having a flash boiler, these cars were the most advanced steamers of their day.

Middle Right: Scott Russell's Steam Carriage, Scotland, 1845.

Bottom: 1895 Hartley Steam Fourseater, Hartley Power Supply Co., Chicago, IL.

PLATE 2

Top: Early steam carriage built by Col. Francis Maceroni and John Squire, which began a shuttle service between Paddington and Edgeware in London on July 18, 1833. Both men had previous association with Goldsworth Gurney, a steam propulsion pioneer.

Bottom: 1897 Columbia Electric Motor Carriage, Pope Manufacturing Co., Hartford, Connecticut. Powered by storage batteries, this vehicle had a top speed of 12-15 mph. on a level surface.

PLATE 3

During the 1890s, France was leading the world in automotive development. Shown here are two examples of 2-cylinder, chain-drive motor carriages built by the Panhard et Levassor firm of Paris.

Top: 1895 4-seater, Forme Mylord, with engine in the rear.

Bottom: 1895 Phaeton 2-seater, with top. This vehicle has the vertical, front-mounted engine, sliding-gear transmission, and rear-wheel drive layout pioneered by Panhard, which became known as la Systeme Panhard.

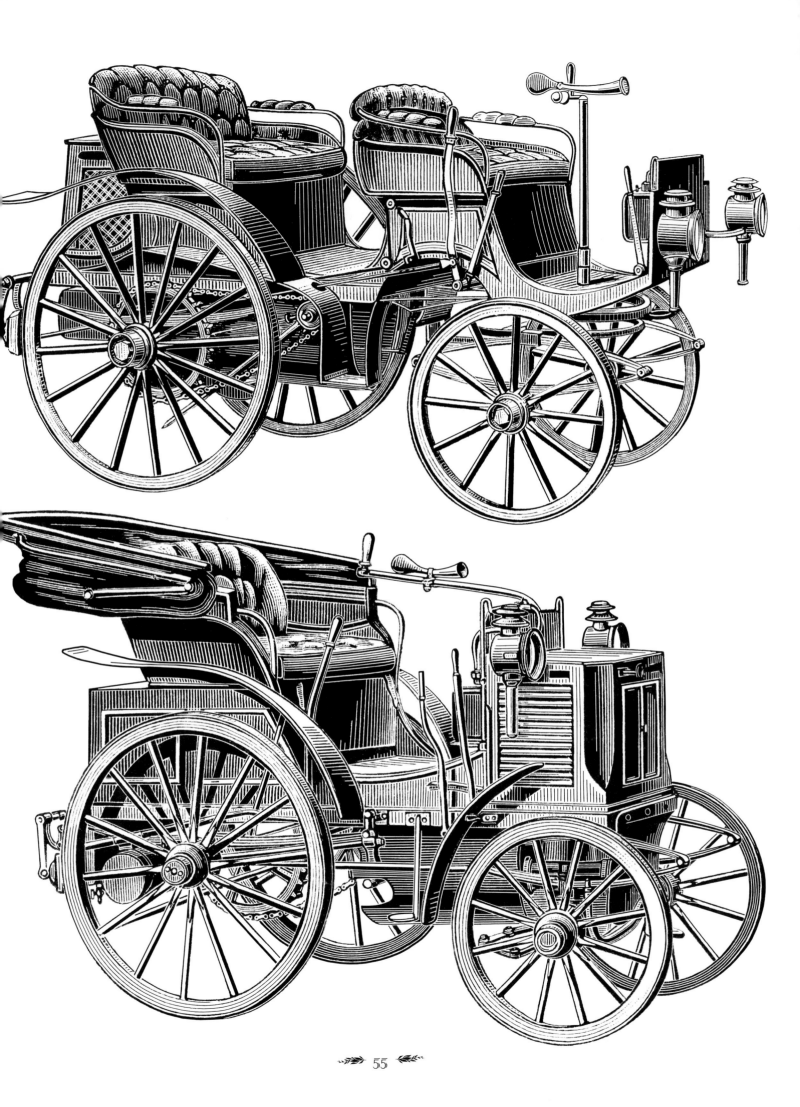

PLATE 4

Two contestants in Chicago's historic *Times-Herald* race of Nov. 28, 1895:

Top: De La Vergne 2-passenger vehicle powered by an imported Benz engine, De La Vergne Refrigerating Co., New York, NY.

Bottom: Oscar Mueller's 4-passenger carriage powered by an imported Benz engine, H. Mueller Manufacturing Co., Chicago, IL. Aside from the winning Duryea, Mueller's was the only other vehicle to complete the icy course. However, Mueller himself only finished the race as an unconscious passenger. He had passed out from exposure and the race umpire, Charles Brady King, took over, finished the race while holding on to Mueller with one arm.

"ENGINEER"

"ENGINEER"

PLATE 5

Top: 1903 Thomas Model 18 1-cylinder, 8-hp Tonneau, priced at $1,400, E.R. Thomas Motor Co., Buffalo, NY.

Upper Middle Center: 1902 Knox Model C 1-cylinder, 8-hp air-cooled Runabout, priced at $1,000, Knox Automobile Co., Springfield, Massachusetts. The engine of this car was in the rear. The front part could be opened out to provide two more seats.

Middle Right: 1903 Rambler 1-cylinder, 6-hp Runabout, priced at $750, Thomas B. Jeffery & Co., Kenosha, Wisconsin. Rambler built 1,350 cars that year, placing it fifth in the industry.

Bottom: 1901 1-cylinder, 6.5-hp Darracq car with shaft-drive and 3-speed column gearshift, Automobiles Darracq S.A., Suresnes, France. Alexandre Darracq, the company's founder, had gotten into car production after selling off his Gladiator Bicycle firm.

DARRACQ

PLATE 6

Top Left: 1903 Pierce 2-cylinder, 15-hp Tonneau, priced at $2,500, The George N. Pierce Co., Buffalo, NY.

Top right: 1902 Columbia Electric Stanhope Phaeton, Electric Vehicle Co., Hartford, CT.

Middle Right: 1902 Columbia Electric Surrey.

Bottom: 1903 Mercedes 4-cylinder, 120-hp Racing Car, Daimler Motoren Gesellschaft, Unterturckheim, Germany. This car had double chain drive with four forward speeds and one reverse. At its wheel is the famous Belgian racing driver Camille Jenatzy, who won the 1903 Gordon Bennett Trophy competition in County Kildare, Ireland. Daimler changed the name of its car from Daimler to Mercedes in 1901 at the behest of Emile Jellinek, the company's agent in Nice. He suggested that the Daimler name sounded too Germanic, and as a substitute he suggested the name of his daughter, Mercedes. There was a separate British-owned Daimler company that continued to market its car as the Daimler. The firms of Daimler and Benz merged in 1926 to become Daimler-Benz AG, their car becoming the Mercedes-Benz.

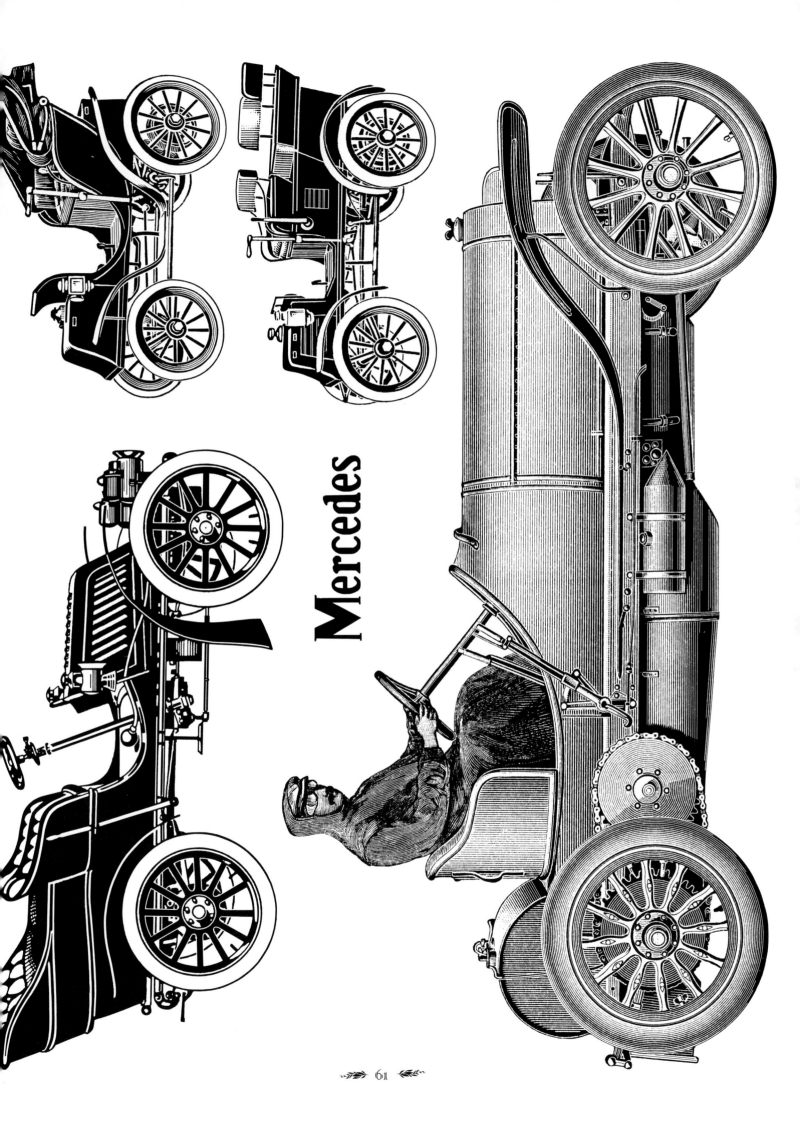

Mercedes

PLATE 7

Top: 1904 Crestmobile Model D 1-cylinder, 8.5-hp Tonneau, priced at $900, Crest Manufacturing Co, Cambridge, MA.

Middle left: 1906 Pope-Waverly Electric Stanhope, Pope Motor Car Co., Indianapolis, IN.

Middle center: 1905 Oldsmobile Model "B" 1-cylinder, 7-hp Curved Dash Runabout, priced at $650, Olds Motor Works, Detroit, MI. This was the car made popular in the song, "My Merry Oldsmobile." Oldsmobile produced 6,500 cars in 1905, the highest in the industry.

Middle right: 1906 Pope-Waverly Electric Station Wagon.

Bottom: 1905 Pope-Hartford Model B 1-cylinder, 10-hp Tonneau, Pope Manufacturing Co., Hartford, CT.

PLATE 8

Top: 1905 Ford Model F, 2-cylinder, 10-hp Touring Car, Ford Motor Co., Detroit, MI.

Middle left: 1906 Pope-Waverly Electric Speed Road Wagon, Pope Motor Car Co., Indianapolis, IN.

Middle center: 1906 Pope-Waverly Electric Physicians Road Wagon.

Middle right: 1906 Pope-Waverly Electric Surrey.

Bottom: 1905 Rambler Type 1, 2-cylinder, 18-hp Surrey, Thomas B. Jeffery & Co., Kenosha, WI. Rambler production that year was 3,807 cars, third highest in the industry.

PLATE 9

Cars from 1906:

Top: Pierce Great Arrow 7-passenger, 40 to 45-hp Touring Car, priced at $5,000, The George N. Pierce Co., Buffalo, NY.

Middle: Thomas Flyer 4-cylinder, 50-hp Touring Car., E.R. Thomas Motor Co., Buffalo, NY.

Bottom: Smith 4-cylinder, 24-hp Side Door Tonneau, priced at $2,500, Smith Automobile Co., Topeka, KS.

PLATE 10

~~❧ 68 ❧~~

Cars from 1907:

Top: Pope-Hartford 4-cylinder, 25 to 30-hp Model L Runabout, priced at $2,750, Pope Manufacturing Co., Hartford, CT.

Middle left: Pope-Toledo 4-cylinder, 50-hp Type XV Runabout, priced at $4,250, Pope Motor Car Co., Toledo, OH.

Bottom: Queen 28, 4-cylinder Touring Car, priced at $2,350, C.H. Blomstrom Motor Co., Detroit, MI.

PLATE 11

Top left: 1907 Rolls-Royce 6-cylinder, 40 to 50-hp Silver Ghost Limousine, Rolls-Royce Ltd., Manchester, England. This company was formed in 1904 by the partnership between Henry Royce, an engineer who wanted to build cars, and Charles Rolls who was one of England's first automobile dealers. The Silver Ghost, first produced in 1907, became known for its quietness.

Top right: 1907 Mitchell Model F, 4-cylinder, 35-hp Touring Car, priced at $2,000, Mitchell Motor Car Co., Racine, WI.

Middle left: 1908 Locomobile Model I, 4-cylinder, 40-hp Runabout, priced at $4,750, Locomobile Co. of America, Bridgeport, CT.

Middle right: 1908 Palmer-Singer Six-50, 6-cylinder, 50-hp Gentleman's Racing Car, priced at $2,450, Palmer & Singer Manufacturing Co. Long Island City, NY.

Bottom: Packard 30, 4-cylinder, 30-hp Touring Car, priced at $4,200, Packard Motor Car Co., Detroit, MI.

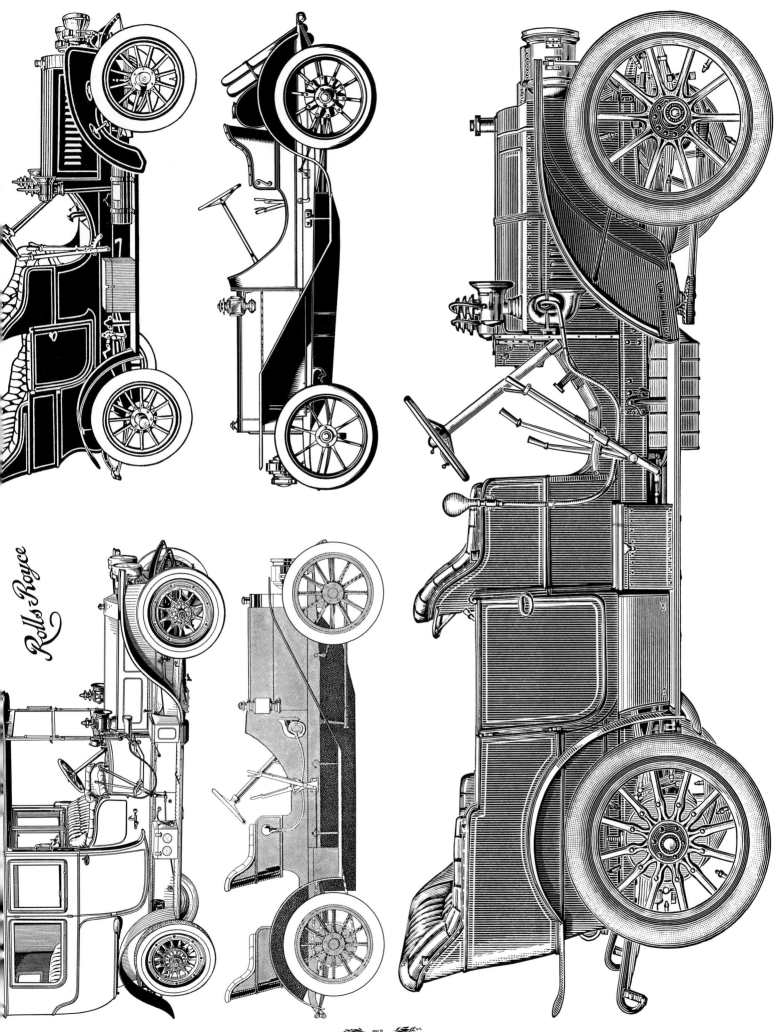

Rolls-Royce

PLATE 12

~ 72 ~

Cars from 1908:

Top: Packard 30, 4-cylinder, 30-hp Limousine, priced at $5,500, Packard Motor Car Co., Detroit, MI.

Middle: Studebaker Model H, 4-cylinder, 30-hp Touring Car, Studebaker Automobile Co., South Bend, IN. Studebaker ranked third in US production that year, building 8,132 cars.

Bottom: Packard 30, 4-cylinder, 30-hp Touring Car with Victoria top.

PLATE 13

Top: 1909 International 2-cylinder, 14-hp Auto Buggy, priced at $850, International Harvester Co., Akron, OH.

Middle left: 1909 Velie Model A, 4-cylinder, 30 to 35-hp Touring Car, priced at $1,750, Velie Motor Vehicle Co., Moline, IL.

Middle right: 1909 Maxwell Junior Model A, 2-cylinder, 10-hp Runabout, priced at $500, Maxwell-Briscoe Motor Co., Tarrytown, NY. Maxwell production that year was 9,460 cars, third in the industry.

Bottom: 1908 Cameron Model 6, 4-cylinder, 20-hp Runabout, priced at $850, Cameron Car Co., Beverly, MA.

PLATE 14

Cars from 1909:

Top: Pierce-Arrow 7-passenger Landaulet (model unknown), The George N. Pierce Co., Buffalo, NY. Later on that year the company name was changed to The Pierce-Arrow Motor Car Co.

Middle left: Lambert No. 19, 4-cylinder, 35 to 40-hp Touring Car, Buckeye Manufacturing Co., Anderson, IN. The Lambert was among the few of its time having a friction drive transmission.

Middle right: Pierce-Arrow Model 24, 4-cylinder, 24-hp, 5-passenger Landaulet, priced at $3,950.

Bottom: Pierce Arrow Model 48, 6-cylinder, 48-hp Touring Car, priced at $5,000.

PLATE 15

Top: Cars from 1909:

Top left: Selden Model 29 Touring Car, Selden Motor Vehicle Co., Rochester, NY.

Top right: Peerless Landaulet, Peerless Motor Car Co., Cleveland, OH. This car was offered in two versions: the 4 cylinder, 30-hp Model 19, and the 6-cylinder, 50-hp Model 25.

Middle left: Speedwell 40-45-hp Double Rumble Roadster, priced at $2,500, Speedwell Motor Car Co., Dayton, OH.

Middle right: Hupmobile Model 20 Runabout, priced at $750, Hupp Motor Car Co., Detroit, MI.

Bottom: Buick Model 17, 4-cylinder, 32.4-hp Touring Car, priced at $1,750, Buick Motor Co., Flint, MI. Buick produced 14,606 cars that year, second only to Ford.

PLATE 16

Cars from 1910:

Top: Black Crow 4-cylinder, 25-hp Model C Roadster, priced at $1,000, Black Manufacturing Co., Chicago, IL

Upper middle center: Starr Runabout, Starr Motor Car Co., Minneapolis, MN. These were intended for production in 4-cylinder, 24-hp and 6-cylinder, 36-hp models. However, very few were ever built.

Lower middle left: Cole Series 30, Model E Flyer Roadster, Priced at $1,500, Cole Motor Car Co., Indianapolis, IN.

Lower middle right: Brush Model D, two-passenger Runabout, priced at $485, Brush Runabout Co., Detroit, MI.

Bottom: Maxwell Model Q-11 Roadster, Maxwell-Briscoe Motor Co., Tarrytown, NY.

PLATE 17

Top: 1910 Cadillac Model 30, 4-cylinder, 33-hp, 5-passenger Touring Car, priced at $1,600, Cadillac Automobile Co., Detroit, MI. Cadillac ranked fifth in the industry that year, producing 10,039 cars.

Middle left: 1910 Cole Series 30, Model G, 4-cylinder, 30-hp, 5-passenger Touring Car, priced at $1,500, Cole Motor Car Co., Indianapolis, IN.

Middle right: 1911 Hupp-Yeats electric 3-Passenger Landaulet, priced at $1,750, R.C.H. Corporation, Detroit, MI. This company was established by Robert Hupp after his departure from the Hupmobile firm.

Bottom: 1910 Hudson Model 20, 4-cylinder, 20-hp, 3-passenger Open Roadster, priced at $900, Hudson Motor Car Co., Detroit, MI.

PLATE 18

⟶ 84 ⟵

Cars from 1911:

Top: Thomas 6-cylinder Limousine, E.R. Thomas Co, Buffalo, NY. At this time the company offered two different 6-cylinder limousines, a 43-hp, 125-inch wheelbase model priced at $5,000 and and a 72-hp, 140-inch wheelbase version priced at $7,500.

Bottom: Case "Fore-Door," 4-cylinder, 30-hp, 5-passenger Touring Car, priced at $1,850, J.I. Case Threshing Machine Co., Racine, WI.

THOMAS

CASE

PLATE 19

Cars from 1911:

Top: Packard Model 30, 4-cylinder, 30-hp Coupe, priced at $4,900, Packard Motor Car Co., Detroit, MI. The horizontally split windshield, common at this time, could be opened out to provide ventilation.

Middle left: Abbott-Detroit Model B, 4-cylinder, 30-hp Touring Car, priced at $1,500, Abbott Motor Car Co., Detroit, MI.

Middle Right: Marmon Model 32, 4-cylinder, 32-hp Touring Car, Nordyke & Marmon Co., Indianapolis, IN.

Bottom: Abbott-Detroit Model B, 4-cylinder, 30-hp Coupe, priced at $2,350.

Abbott

Detroit

PLATE 20

Cars from 1911:

Top: Cartercar Model H, 4-cylinder, 30-hp Roadster, priced at $1,150, Cartercar Co., Pontiac, MI. The Cartercar became known for its friction drive transmission. The firm's founder, Byron J. Carter, died in 1908 of injuries sustained while assisting a woman by cranking her stalled car. The crank handle kicked back, breaking Carter's jaw, and then gangrene set in. He had been a friend of Henry Leland of Cadillac, and this became the impetus for Leland's efforts to develop an electrical starter, finally achieved with help from Charles F. Kettering of Delco.

Middle: Bergdoll 30 "Louis J," 4-cylinder, 30-hp Roadster, Louis J. Bergdoll Motor Co., Philadelphia.

Bottom: Abbott-Detroit Model B, 4-cylinder, 30-hp Roadster, priced at $1,500, Abbott Motor Car Co., Detroit, MI.

PLATE 21

Cars from 1912:

Top: Stevens-Duryea Model AA, 6-cylinder, 43.8 hp, 7-passenger Touring Car, priced at $3,900, Stevens-Duryea Co., Chicopee Falls, MA. J. Frank Duryea, one of the famous Duryea brothers, founded this company in partnership with J. Stevens Arms & Tool Co.

Middle: Rambler Cross Country 4-cylinder, 38-hp Touring Car, priced at $1,650, Thomas B. Jeffery Co., Kenosha, WI. Jeffery subsequently discontinued the Rambler and built the Jeffery car into 1916. The firm was bought out in 1916 by Charles W. Nash.

Bottom: Ford Model T, 4-cylinder, 20-hp Touring Car, priced at $690, Ford Motor Co. Detroit, MI. Ford ranked first in U.S. production that year, building 78,440 cars.

PLATE 22

Cars from 1912:

Top: Maxwell "Mascotte" 4-cylinder Touring Car, Maxwell-Briscoe Motor Co., Tarrytown, NY. At this time Maxwell-Briscoe had become part of United States Motor Co., a conglomerate formed by Maxwell partner Benjamin Briscoe. Other companies involved included Brush, Stoddard-Dayton, and Columbia. Unfortunately this conglomerate quickly collapsed. With the help of Walter Flanders, Jonathan Maxwell managed to save his company, relocating it to Detroit in 1913. In 1914 Briscoe formed a new company under his own name.

Middle: Franklin Model D Touring Car, Franklin Automobile Co., Syracuse, NY. This air-cooled car was priced at $3,500.

Bottom: White Model 60, 6-cylinder Touring Car, The White Co., Cleveland, OH. Although it had a crank, this car was also equipped with an electrical starter.

PLATE 23

Cars from 1912:

Top: White Model 60, 6-cylinder, 7-passenger Touring Car, priced at $5,000, The White Co., Cleveland, OH.

Middle left: Abbott-Detroit Model C, 4-cylinder, 44-hp Limousine, priced at $3,000, Abbott Motor Car Co., Detroit, MI. Like the White, this car also offered electrical starting.

Middle right: Haynes Model 21, 4-cylinder, 40-hp, 5-Passenger Touring Car, priced at $2,100, Haynes Automobile Co., Kokomo, IN.

Bottom: Pratt Forty, 4-cylinder, 40-hp Touring Car, priced at $2,100, Elkhart Carriage & Harness Manufacturing Co., Elkhart, IN.

PLATE 24

Cars from 1912:

Top: Correja Model R Six, 60-hp Roadster, priced at $1,950, Vandewater & Co. Ltd., Elizabeth, NJ. The company slogan was "Takes Every Hill and Always Will."

Middle: Regal Model N, 4-cylinder, 25-hp Roadster with underslung suspension, priced at $900, Regal Motor Car Co., Detroit, MI. Regal was a modestly successful firm until World War I shortages led to its demise.

Bottom: Moline Model M-35, 4-cylinder, Dreadnought Roadster, priced at $1,700, Moline Automobile Co., East Moline, IL.

PLATE 25

Top left: 1912 Cadillac 4-cylinder, 40-hp Limousine, priced at $3,250, Cadillac Automobile Co., Detroit, MI.

Top right: 1912 Stoddard Dayton 4-cylinder, 48-hp, 7-passenger Saybrook Limousine, priced at $3,900, Stoddard-Dayton Division of United States Motor Co., Dayton, OH.

Middle left: 1912 Studebaker Flanders "20" Touring Car, Studebaker Automobile Co., South Bend, IN. In 1911 Studebaker terminated a relationship with Garford for providing it cars and acquired the E-M-F company. It had marketed E-M-F cars since 1908, and the Flanders model was an E-M-F carryover.

Middle right: 1912 Overland Model 60 4-cylinder 35-hp Touring Car, priced at $1,200, Willys-Overland Co., Toledo, OH. Willys-Overland produced 28,572 cars that year, ranking it second behind Ford.

Bottom: 1913 Lozier 6-cylinder, 51.6-hp Lakewood Touring Car, priced at $5,000, Lozier Motor Co., Detroit, MI.

PLATE 26

Top: 1913 Kissel Kar Model H-13, 4-cylinder, 32.4-hp Touring Car, priced at $2,000, Kissel Motor Car Co., Hartford, WI.

Middle: 1913 Packard "48-Six," 6-cylinder, 48-hp Touring Car, Packard Motor Car Co., Detroit, MI.

Bottom: 1912 Peerless "38-Six," 6-cylinder, 38-hp Limousine, priced at $5,000, Peerless Motor Car Co., Cleveland, OH.

PLATE 27

Cars from 1913:

Top: Pope-Hartford Model 29, 6-cylinder, 60-hp Touring Car, priced at $4,250, Pope Manufacturing Co., Hartford, CT.

Middle: Peerless "48-Six" 6-cylinder, 48.6-hp Touring Car, priced at $5,000, Peerless Motor Car Co., Cleveland, OH.

Bottom: Packard "38," 6-cylinder, 38-hp Landaulet, priced at $5,300, Packard Motor Car Co., Detroit, MI.

PLATE 28

Cars from 1913:

Top: Apperson "Jack Rabbit," 4-cylinder Roadster, Apperson Brothers Automobile Co., Kokomo, IN. This car came in two models. The 45-hp version sold for $1,600 and the 55-hp version for $2,000.

Middle: Imperial 34 4-cylinder 40-hp Touring Car, priced at $1,450, Imperial Automobile Co., Jackson, MI.

Bottom: K-R-I-T Model KT, 4-cylinder, 25-hp, 5-passenger Touring Car, priced at $900, Krit Motor Car Co., Detroit, MI. This company's logo was a swastika.

PLATE 29

Cars from 1913:

Top: Detroit Electric Clear Vision Brougham, Anderson Electric Car Co., Detroit, MI. Based on the wheelbase length, there were four different models of this car.

Bottom: Overland Model 69, 4-cylinder, 25.6-hp, 5-passenger Touring Car, priced at $985, Willys-Overland Co., Toledo, OH. Overland ranked second in U.S. auto production for 1913, building 37,422 cars.

Overland

Detroit

PLATE 30

Cars from 1913:

Top: King "36," 4-cylinder, 36-hp Roadster, priced at $1,190, King Motor Car Co., Detroit, Michigan. This company was founded by Charles Brady King in 1911, but he left it in 1912. King was famous for a number of things, including building and driving the first motor vehicle in Detroit in 1896, and inventing the jackhammer. He was an interesting and multifaceted individual, being an engineer, inventor, soldier, artist, etcher, musician, architect, poet, and mystic.

Middle left: Napier 6-cylinder car with coachwork by Cunard, D. Napier & Sons Ltd., Acton, West London, England. Advertised as "The Noiseless Napier" this car was built for the elite. Besides various lords, earls, dukes and viscounts, its clientele included Lloyd George, Winston Churchill, A.J. Balfour, and Andrew Carnegie. In 1904, Napier became first in the world to offer a serially produced 6-cylinder car.

Middle right: American Underslung "American Tourist" Model 34-A, 4-cylinder, 50-hp, 4-passenger Touring Car, priced at $2,350, American Motors Co., Indianapolis, IN.

Bottom: Argo Electric Model B Roadster, priced at $2,500, Argo Electric Vehicle Co., Saginaw, MI.

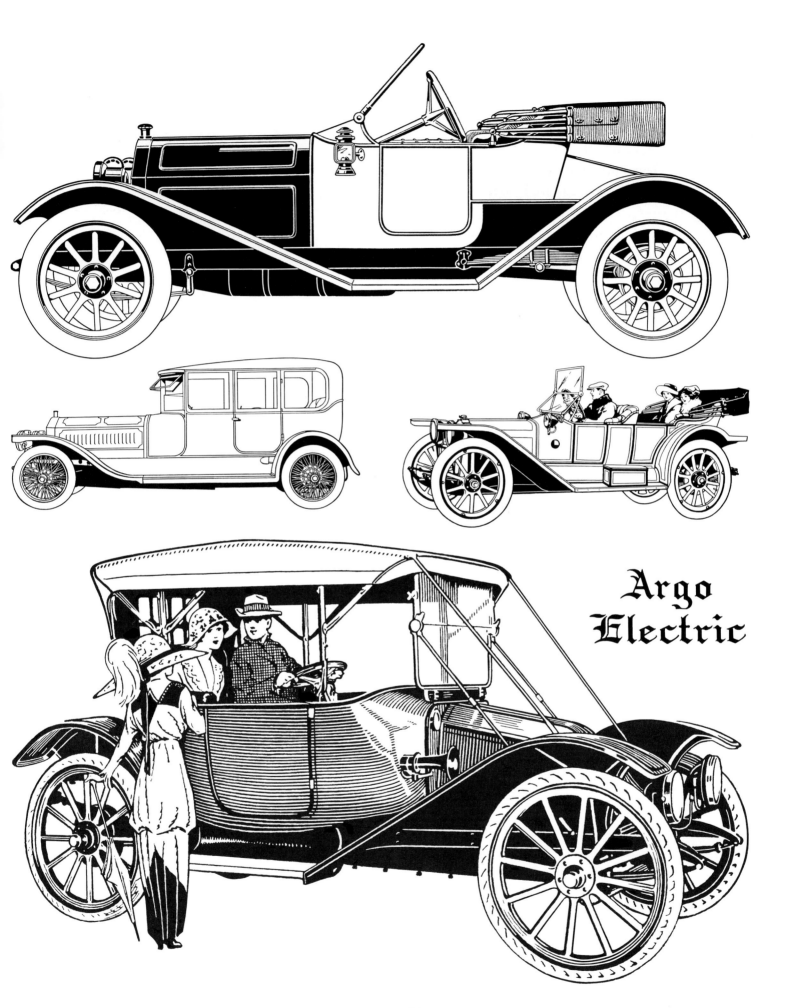

Argo
Electric

PLATE 31

Cars from 1914:

Top: Hudson 6-cylinder, 54-hp, 7-passenger Touring Car, priced at $2250, Hudson Motor Car Co., Detroit, MI.

Middle left: Mitchell Little Six, 43.8-hp, 4 or 5-passenger Touring Car, priced at $1,895, Mitchell-Lewis Motor Car Co., Racine, WI.

Middle Right: Locomobile 6-cylinder Opera Berline, Locomobile Co. of America, Bridgeport, CT. This is likely the 48.6-hp, 140-inch wheelbase version of the car.

Bottom: Mitchell Little Six, 43.8-hp, 7-passenger Touring Car, priced at $1,995.

PLATE 32

Cars from 1914:

Top: Stutz Torpedo Roadster, Stutz Motor Car Co., Indianapolis, IN. This car came in 4-cylinder, 50-hp, and 6-cylinder, 55-hp versions, priced at $2,000 and $2,250, respectively. It differed from the Bearcat model mainly in that its coachwork included cowling and doors.

Middle left: Oakland Touring Car (model unknown), Oakland Motor Car Co., Pontiac, MI.

Bottom: Pioneer Cycle Car, priced at $385, The American Manufacturing Co., Chicago, IL. This lightweight 2-cylinder, air-cooled car had 12 to 15-hp. Cyclecars became a fad in the 1910-16 period, and about 125 different brands were built.

PLATE 33

Cars from 1914:

Top: Winton Model 20, 6-cylinder, 48.6-hp Touring Car, Winton Motor Car Co., Cleveland, OH.

Middle left: Seabrook R.M.C., 4-cylinder Touring Car with underslung suspension. This car, marketed by the Seabrook Brothers in London, was an export from America's Regal Motor Car Co., Detroit, MI.

Middle right: Lozier Light Four, 28.9-hp Touring Car, priced at $2,100, Lozier Motor Co., Detroit. At this time the company was in trouble and they had turned to making cheaper models.

Bottom: Reo (the Fifth), 4-cylinder, 30 to 35-hp, 5-passenger Touring Car, priced at $1,175, Reo Motor Car Co., Lansing, MI. The letters in "Reo" stood for the initials of Ransom E. Olds, the founder of Oldsmobile and later of Reo. Reo built 13,516 cars that year, placing it sixth in U.S. production.

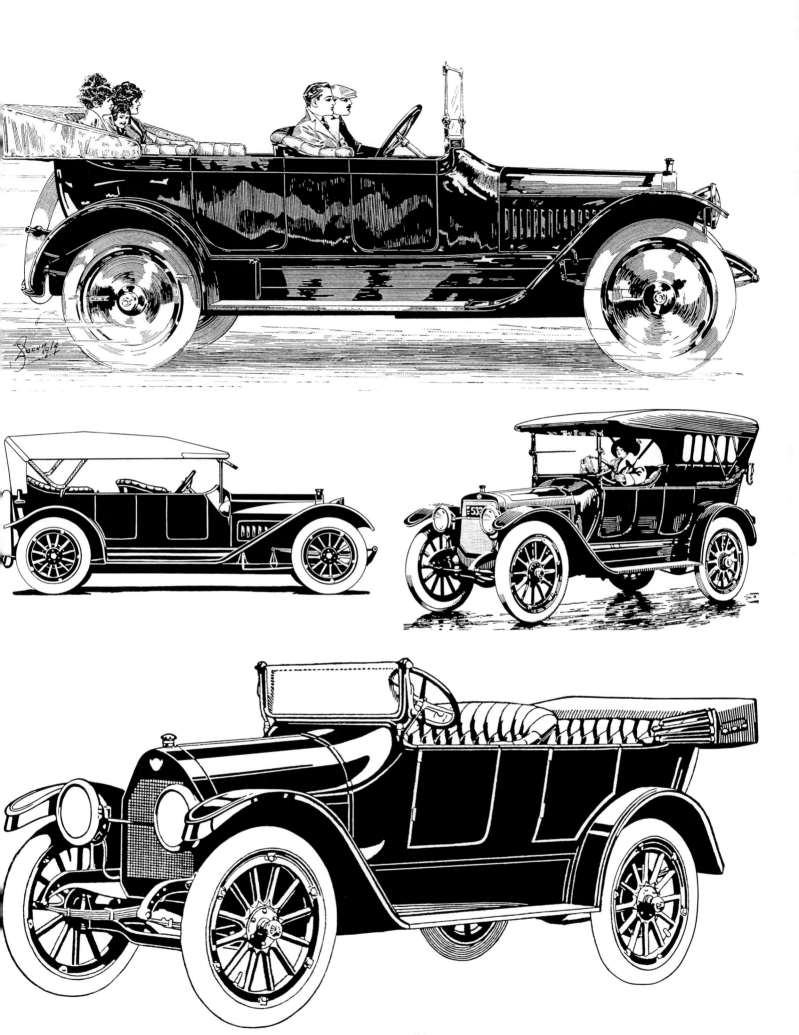

PLATE 34

Cars from 1914:

Top: National Series V, 4-cylinder, 40-hp, 128-inch wheelbase, 7-passenger Touring Car, priced at $3,400, National Motor Vehicle Co., Indianapolis, IN .

Middle: National Six, 34-hp, 132-inch wheelbase, 5-passenger Touring Car, priced at $2,375. National gained a lot of publicity in 1912 when one of their cars won the Indianapolis 500, but afterwards they dropped their racing program.

Bottom: Moon Light Six-50, 33.7-hp, 132-inch wheelbase Touring Car, Moon Motor Car Co., St. Louis, MO.

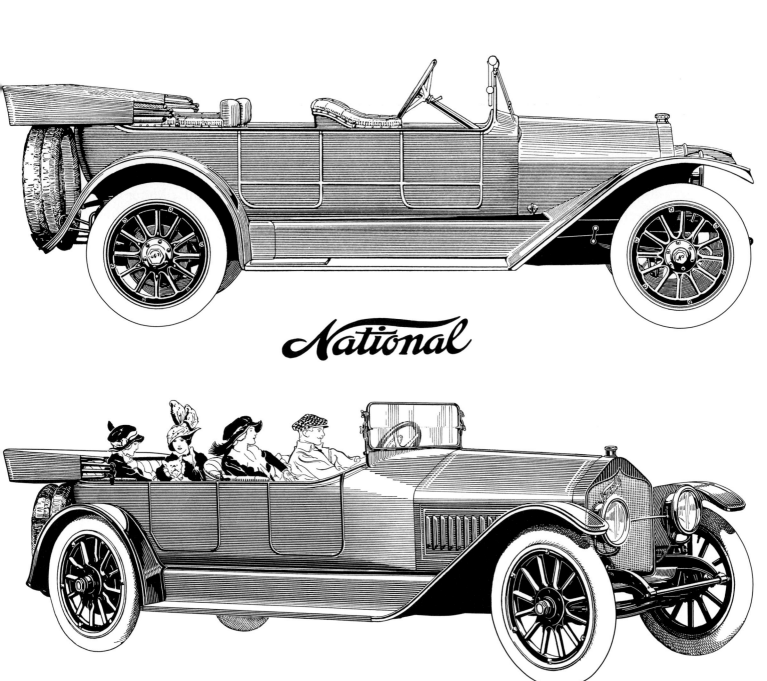

National

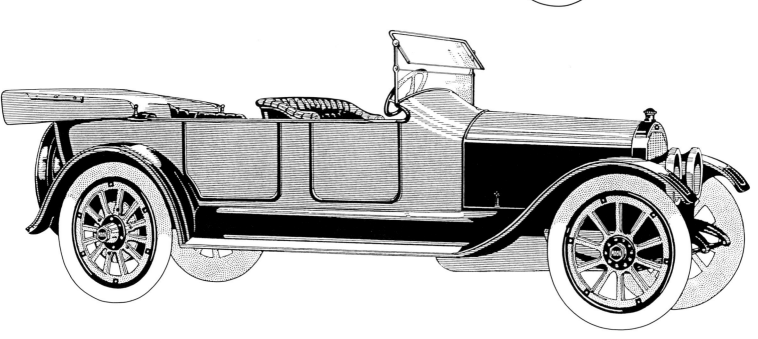

PLATE 35

Cars from 1915:

Top: Cadillac V-8, 77-hp, 7-passenger Touring Car, priced at $1,975, Cadillac Motor Car Co., Detroit, MI. Cadillac ranked seventh in U.S. auto production that year, building 20,404 cars.

Middle left: Chalmers Light Six, 48-hp Touring Car, priced at $1,650, Chalmers Motor Car Co., Detroit, MI.

Middle right: Detroiter Model C-5, 4-cylinder, 20-hp, 5-passenger Touring Car, priced at $1,050, Briggs-Detroiter Co., Detroit, MI.

Lower middle right: Peerless Model 55, 6-cylinder, 29.4-hp, 5-passenger Touring Car, priced at $2,250, Peerless Motor Car Co., Cleveland, Ohio.

Bottom: Cadillac V-8, 77-hp, 7-passenger Limousine, priced at $3,450.

PLATE 36

Cars from 1915:

Top: Abbott-Detroit Eight-80, V-8, 80-hp Touring Car, priced at $1,950, The Consolidated Car Co., Detroit, MI.

Middle left: Hupmobile Sedan, Hupp Motor Car Co., Detroit, MI.

Middle right: Ford Model T, 4-cylinder, 20-hp Coupelet, priced at $750, Ford Motor Co., Detroit, MI. Ford built 435,898 cars that year, once again ranking it first in the industry.

Bottom: Winton Six Limousine, Winton Motor Car Co., Cleveland, OH.

WINTON
SIX

PLATE 37

Cars from 1916:

Top left: Chandler Six, 27-hp Limousine, priced at $2,450, Chandler Motor Car Co., Cleveland, OH. Chandler was founded in 1913 by a group of managerial people formerly with Lozier.

Middle: Chalmers 6-cylinder Touring Car (model unknown), Chalmers Motor Car, Co., Detroit, MI.

Bottom: Moon Touring Car (model unknown), Moon Motor Car Co., St. Louis, MO.

Chalmers

PLATE 38

Cars from 1916:

Top: Oldsmobile Light Eight Model 44, V-8, 40-hp Touring Car, priced at $1,195, Olds Motor Works, Lansing, MI.

Middle left: Kissell Kar Model 4-32, 4-cylinder, 24-hp Touring Car, priced at $1,050, Kissell Motor Car Co., Hartford, WI.

Middle right: Pullman 4-cylinder Touring Car, priced at $740, Pullman Motor Car Co., York, PA.

Bottom: Paige Touring Car (model unknown), Paige-Detroit Motor Car Co., Detroit, MI. Paige's company slogan was "The most beautiful car in America."

PLATE 39

Cars from 1916:

Top: Hudson Super-Six, 76-hp, 7-passenger Phaeton, priced at $1,375, Hudson Motor Car Co, Detroit, MI.

Bottom: Front end of King Model D, V-8 (model unknown) priced at $1,350, King Motor Car Co., Detroit, MI.

PLATE 40

Cars from 1917:

Top: Studebaker 7-passenger Touring Car, Studebaker Automobile Co., South Bend, IN. This car was offered in 4- and 6-cylinder models. Studebaker ranked seventh in U.S. Auto production that year, building 39,686 cars.

Middle: Chalmers 6-cylinder, 30-hp, 7-passenger Touring Car, priced at $1,350, Chalmers Motor Car Co., Detroit, MI. At this time Chalmers was building around 20,000 cars per year. However, it got into trouble in the postwar recession and was taken over in 1922 by Maxwell.

Bottom: Roamer 5-passenger, 6-cylinder, 23-hp Touring Car, priced at $1,850, Barley Motor Car Co., Streator, IL. For its radiator design, Roamer borrowed from Rolls-Royce and its company slogan became "America's Smartest Car."

PLATE 41

Cars from 1917:

Top: Mitchell Model C-42, 6-cylinder, 29.4-hp, 7-passenger Touring Car, priced at $1,460, Mitchell Motors Co., Racine, WI.

Middle: Maxwell Model 25, 4-cylinder, 21-hp Roadster, priced at $635, Maxwell Motor Co., Detroit. Maxwell built 75,000 cars that year, ranking it sixth in U.S. production.

Bottom: Saxon Model B5R, 4-cylinder, 12.1-hp Roadster, priced at $815, Saxon Motor Car Corporation, Detroit, MI.

PLATE 42

Top: 1917 Premier Model 6B, 6-cylinder, 27.34-hp Touring Car, priced at $1,895, Premier Motor Car Co., Indianapolis, IN.

Middle Left: 1918 Pierce-Arrow Model 48, 6-cylinder, 48.6-hp French Brougham, The Pierce-Arrow Motor Car Co., Buffalo, NY.

Middle Right: 1918 Nash Six, 55-hp Touring Car, Nash Motors Co., Kenosha, WI. In 1916, Charles W. Nash, a former president of Buick, bought out the Thomas B. Jeffery Co., previous maker of Rambler cars and later Jeffery cars and trucks, and established the Nash Co.

Bottom: 1918 Milburn Light Electric Brougham, priced at $1,885, The Milburn Wagon Co, Toledo, OH.

PLATE 43

Cars from 1918:

Top: Hudson Super Six, 76-hp Runabout Landau, priced at $2,350, Hudson Motor Car Co., Detroit, MI.

Middle left: Pierce-Arrow Model 48, 6-cylinder, 48.6-hp Coupe, The Pierce-Arrow Motor Car Co., Buffalo, NY.

Middle Right: Pierce-Arrow Model 48, 6-cylinder, 48.6-hp Brougham.

Bottom: Hudson Super Six, 76-hp Touring Limousine, priced at $3,150.

PLATE 44

Cars from 1918:

Top: Marmon 34, 6-cylinder, 74-hp Touring Car, Nordyke & Marmon Co., Indianapolis, IN.

Middle: Buick Model E Six-44, 60-hp Roadster, priced at $1,265, Buick Motor Co., Flint, MI. Buick produced 77,691 cars that year, ranking it fourth in the industry.

Bottom: Stephens Salient Six, 25.3-hp Touring Car with Victoria top, priced at $1,485, Stephens Motor Branch of Moline Plow Co., Freeport, IL.

STEPHENS *Salient Six*

PLATE 45

Cars from 1918:

Top: Cole Series 870 "Aero-Eight" V-8, 39.2-hp, 7-passenger Touring Car, priced at $2,395, Cole Motor Car Co., Indianapolis, IN.

Middle: Case Model U, 6-cylinder, 50-hp, 7-passenger Touring Car, Case Motor Car Division of J.I. Case Threshing Machine Co., Racine, WI.

Bottom: Packard Twin Six, V-12, 90-hp, 7-passenger Limousine, Packard Motor Car Co. Detroit, MI. At this time Packard offered two limousine models plus an Imperial Limousine.

PACKARD TWIN SIX

PLATE 46

Top: 1918 HAL Model 25, V-12, 40-hp Touring Car, priced at $2,600, HAL Motor Car Co., Cleveland, OH. This company was founded by Harry A. Lozier who left his Lozier Motor Co. after being forced by stockholders to build cheaper cars.

Middle: 1918 Hudson Super Six, 76-hp Phaeton, Hudson Motor Car Co., Detroit, MI.

Bottom: 1919 Packard Twin Six, V-12, 90-hp Touring Car, Packard Motor Car Co., Detroit, MI.

PLATE 47

Cars of the Haynes Automobile Co., Kokomo, IN:

Top: 1919 Light Twelve, V-12, 36.3-hp, 4-door Roadster, priced at $3,250.

Middle: 1920 6-cylinder, 50-hp Special Speedster.

Bottom: 1919 Light Twelve, V-12, 36.3-hp, 7-passenger Touring Car, priced at $3,250.

PLATE 48

Jordan 6-cylinder 56-hp cars from 1920, Jordan Motor Car Co., Cleveland, OH:

Top: Silhouette 5-passenger Brougham, priced at $3,600 or $3,800, depending on the wheelbase length.

Middle: Silhouette 5-passenger Touring Car, priced at $2,550.

Bottom: Silhouette 4-door Sedan.

PLATE 49

Cars from 1920:

Top: Bour-Davis 6-cylinder Touring Car, Louisiana Motor Car Co., Shreveport, LA. This car was offered in 42 and 55-hp models. Bour-Davis had been started in Detroit in 1916, moved to Frankfort, IN in 1918, and to Louisiana in 1919. It went out of business in 1922.

Middle: Roamer Model C, 6-cylinder, 54-hp Touring Car, Barley Motor Car Co., Kalamazoo, MI.

Bottom: Cole Aero-Eight, V-8 Sedan (model unknown), Cole Motor Car Co., Indianapolis, IN.

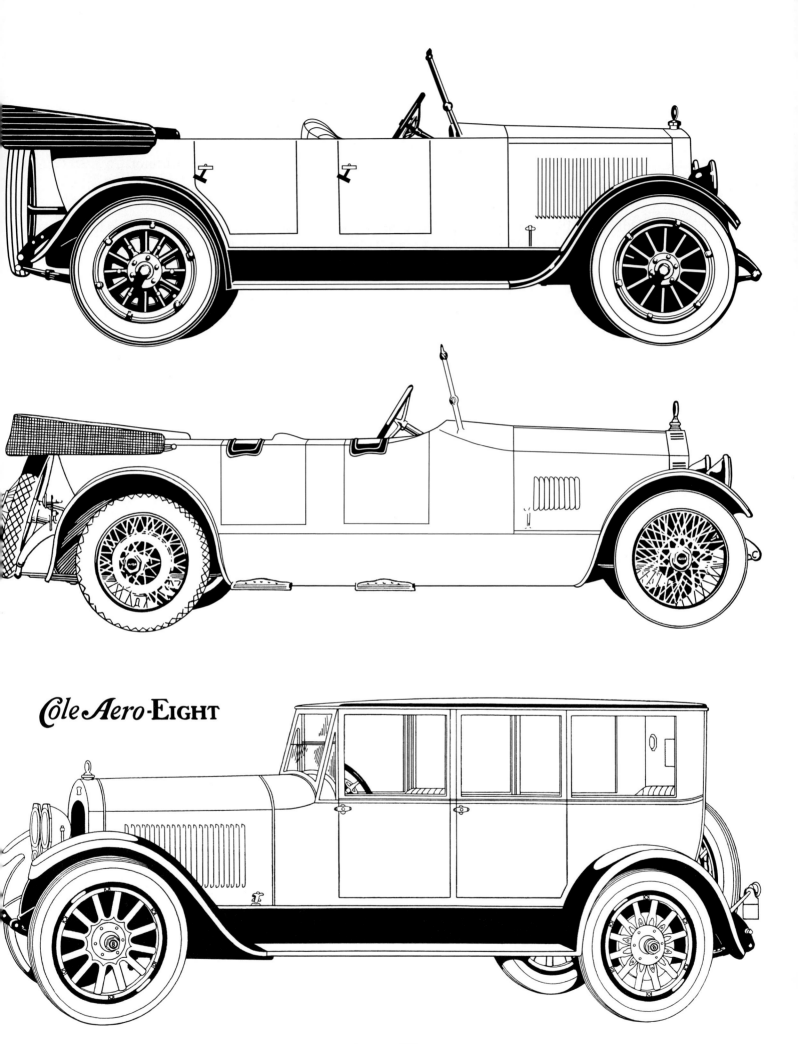

Cole Aero-Eight

PLATE 50

Top: 1920 Severin 6-cylinder, 65-hp Touring Car, priced at $2,400, Severin Motor Co., Kansas City, MO.

Middle left. 1920 Ford Model T, 4-cylinder, 20-hp, 2-door Sedan, priced at $975, Ford Motor Co., Detroit, MI. Once again Ford led U.S. auto production, building 806,040 cars that year.

Middle Right: 1920 Studebaker Model 6EG "Big Six," 60-hp, 7-passenger Touring Car, The Studebaker Corporation of America, South Bend, IN. Studebaker ranked sixth in U.S. auto production that year, building 48,831 cars.

Bottom: 1920 Apperson V-8, 60-hp Touring Car, Apperson Brothers Automobile Co., Kokomo, IN.

APPERSON

PLATE 51

Cars from 1921:

Top: Winton Model 25, 6-cylinder, 70-hp, 7-passenger Touring Car, priced at $4,600, Winton Motor Car Co., Cleveland, OH.

Middle Left: Anderson Model S-40, 6-cylinder, 55-hp Sedan, priced at $3,200, Anderson Motor Co., Rock Hill, South Carolina. A company slogan was "A Little Bit Higher in Price, but Made in Dixie."

Middle right: Mitchell Model F-40, 6-cylinder, 40-hp Roadster, priced at $1,750, Mitchell Motors Co., Racine, WI.

Bottom: Davis Series 50, 6-cylinder, 58-hp, 4-passenger Coupe, priced at $3,085, George W. Davis Motor Car Co., Richmond, IN.

PLATE 52

Cars from 1921:

Top: Dodge Brothers Model 30, 4-cylinder, 35-hp, 5-passenger Touring Car, priced at $1,285, Dodge Brothers, Detroit, MI. The company built 81,000 cars that year, ranking it fourth in the industry.

Middle left: Dixie Flyer Model H, 4-cylinder, 40-hp Roadster, priced a $1,595, Dixie Motor Car Co., Louisville, KY.

Middle right: Dixie Flyer Model H, 4-cylinder, 40-hp, 5-passenger Touring Car, priced at $1,595.

Bottom: Cleveland Six Model 41, 45-hp Touring Car, priced at $1,435, Cleveland Automobile Co., Cleveland, OH. This company had a close relationship with Chandler and used the company's overhead valve six engine.

PLATE 53

Cars from 1922:

Top: 1922 Haynes Model 55, 6-cylinder, 50-hp, 3-passenger Coupelet, Haynes Automobile Co. Kokomo, IN.

Middle left: Chevrolet Model 490, 4-cylinder, 22-hp, 5-passenger Touring Car, priced at $525, Chevrolet Motor Co., Detroit, MI.

Middle right: Citroen 5 CV Torpedo Roadster with boattail styling, S.A. Andre Citroen, Paris. This was one of the earlier models the company built after its factory was converted back from war-time use.

Bottom: Chevrolet Model 490, 4-cylinder, 22-hp, 4-door Sedan, priced at $875. At this time Chevrolet had come under the presidency of William S. Knudsen, formerly Ford's production manager. Chevrolet production that year was 138,932, ranking it third in the industry.

CHEVROLET

PLATE 54

Top: 1923 Hudson Super Six, 76-hp, 2-door Coach, priced at $1,745, Hudson Motor Car Co., Detroit, MI.

Middle: 1922 Allen Artcraft 4-cylinder, 37-hp All-Weather Roadster, priced at $1,845, The Allen Motor Co., Columbus, OH.

Bottom: 1923 Buick Roadster, likely the Model 34, 4-cylinder, 35-hp model priced at $865, Buick Motor Co., Flint, MI.

PLATE 55

Top: 1923 Moon Six-40, 50-hp Touring Car., priced at $1,195, Moon Motor Car Co., St. Louis, MO.

Middle: 1922 Jordan 6-cylinder, 56-hp Playboy Roadster, Jordan Motor Car Co., Cleveland, OH.

Bottom: 1923 Dort Yale 4-cylinder, 32-hp, 5-passenger Sedan, priced at $1,095, Dort Motor Car Co., Flint, MI.

Dort

PLATE 56

Top: 1923 Lincoln Model L, V-8, 90-hp, 7-passenger Touring Car, Lincoln Motor Co., Detroit, MI.

Middle Right: 1922 Wills Sainte Claire V-8 Roadster, C.H. Wills & Co., Marysville, MI. This company was founded by Childe Harold Wills who earlier had been the metallurgical specialist at Ford Motor Co. Wills was a perfectionist who built high quality automobiles. The company symbol was a Canadian Goose.

Bottom: 1923 Lincoln Model L, V-8, 90-hp Holbrook Cabriolet.

PLATE 57

Cars from 1923:

Top: Lincoln Model L, V-8, 90-hp Town Car, Lincoln Motor Co., Detroit, MI.

Upper middle center: Pierce-Arrow Model 33, 6-cylinder Runabout, priced at $5,250, The Pierce-Arrow Motor Car Co., Buffalo, NY.

Lower middle left: Pierce-Arrow Model 33, 6-cylinder, 38-hp Enclosed Drive Limousine, priced at $7,000.

Lower middle right: Maxwell Model 25, 4-cylinder, 30-hp, 5-passenger Touring Car, priced at $885, Maxwell Motor Corporation, Detroit, MI. Maxwell's previous Model 25 cars had gained a reputation for poor engineering. Thus this improved version, built under the leadership of Walter P. Chrysler, was promoted as "The Good Maxwell." Maxwell car production terminated in 1925 after the company was reorganized as the Chrysler Corporation.

Bottom: Lincoln Model L, V-8, 90-hp Judkins Berline.

PLATE 58

Top: 1923 Stutz Special Six, 70-hp, 5-passenger Touring Car, Stutz Motor Car Co., Indianapolis.

Middle: 1924 Pierce-Arrow Model 80, 6-cylinder, 70-hp Touring Car with Victoria top, The Pierce-Arrow Motor Car Co., Buffalo, NY.

Bottom: 1923 Moon Model Six-58, Petite Touring Sedan, priced at $2580, Moon Motor Car Co., St. Louis, MO.

MOON

PLATE 59

Cars from 1924:

Top: Buick 4-cylinder, 35-hp, 5-passenger Sedan, priced at $1,495, Buick Motor Co., Flint, MI. In 1924, Buick ranked fifth in U.S. auto production, building 160,411 cars.

Middle left: Mathis 6-cylinder Roadster, Mathis S.A., Strasbourg, France.

Bottom: Peerless Model 66, V-8, 70-hp, 7-passenger Touring Car, priced at $2,750, Peerless Motor Car Co., Cleveland, OH.

BUICK

PLATE 60

Cars from 1924:

Top: Jewett Six, 50-hp, 5-passenger Special Touring Car, priced at $1,220, Jewett Motors, Inc., Detroit, MI. This company was a subsidiary of Paige-Detroit Motor Car Co., and named after its president.

Middle Left: Buick 6-cylinder, 70-hp Double Service Sedan, priced at $1,695, Buick Motor Co., Flint, MI.

Middle Right: Fiat Model 510, 6-cylinder Brougham, priced at $5,400 (New York), Fiat (Fabbrica Italiana Automobili Torino), Turin, Italy. Fiat was founded on July 11, 1899.

Bottom: Buick 6-cylinder, 70-hp, 7-passenger Touring Car, priced at $1,565.

PLATE 61

Cars from 1924:

Top: Dodge Brothers Special, 4-cylinder, 35-hp, 4-passenger Coupe, priced at $1,535, Dodge Brothers, Detroit, MI. The company built 193,861 cars that year, ranking it third in the industry.

Middle left: Chevrolet Superior Series F, 4-cylinder, 26-hp, 2-passenger Coupe, priced at $490, Chevrolet Motor Co., Detroit, MI.

Middle right: Essex Six Coach, priced at $1,000, Hudson Motor Car Co., Detroit, MI. Combined Hudson/Essex output that year was 133,950 cars, placing it sixth in U.S. production.

Bottom: Auburn English Coach, Auburn Automobile Co., Auburn, IN.

PLATE 62

1925 Jordan cars from the Great Line Eight, 74-hp series, Jordan Motor Car Co., Cleveland, Ohio.

Top: 2-door Sedan, priced at $2,675.

Middle: 5-passenger Touring Car, priced at $2,575.

Bottom: 4-door Sedan, priced at $2,975.

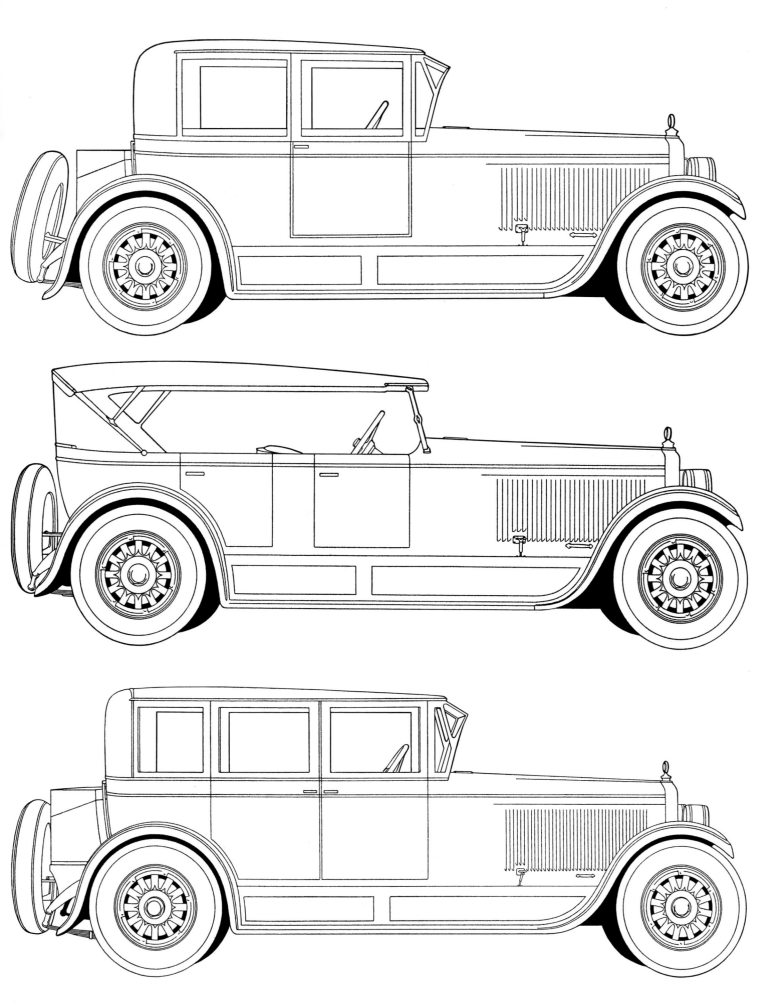

PLATE 63

Top: 1926 Jordan Line Eight, 74-hp Playboy Roadster with rumble seat, priced at $1,695, Jordan Motor Car Co., Cleveland, OH.

Middle left: 1925 Marmon Model 74, 6-cylinder 84-hp Roadster, priced at $3,165, Nordyke & Marmon Co., Indianapolis, IN.

Middle Right: 1926 Ford Model T, 4-cylinder, 20-hp Coupe, Ford Motor Co., Detroit, MI. This illustration from a French advertisement was done by Rene Vincent (1879-1936), a French artist well known for his art deco style. It was rare in the U.S. for artists to sign commercial car illustrations. Ford produced 1,426,612 cars in 1926, once again ranking it first in the industry.

Bottom: Diana 8-cylinder, 72-hp, 2-door Sedan, priced at $2,095, Diana Motors Co., St. Louis, MO. This firm was a subsidiary of Moon Motor Car Co.

PLATE 64

Rolls-Royce cars from 1926 with bodies by the coach-building firm Brewster & Co.

Top: Nottingham.

Middle: Sport Double Enclosed Drive Limousine.

Bottom: Landaulet. At this time Rolls-Royce was built in both Silver Ghost and Phantom I models.

PLATE 65

Top: 1927 Diana Straight Eight, 72-hp "Palm Beach Special" Roadster, Diana Motors Co., St. Louis, MO. The folding rear seat of this car was known as a "rumble seat," or in Englad as a "dickey seat." These were very popular in the 1920s, especially with romantic couples and children. They allowed space for extra passengers, but otherwise provided normal trunk space. The name does not refer to noise, but to a servant's seat above the luggage at the rear of a carriage or stage coach.

Middle left: Wolverine 6-Cylinder Cabriolet, priced at $1,195, Reo Motor Car Co., Lansing, MI. An unrelated Wolverine car was built by Reid Manufacturing Co., of Detroit from 1904-6.

Middle right: 1927 Lincoln, English version, V-8, 90-hp Cabriolet De Ville, by Barker, Lincoln Cars Ltd., Manchester. For selling its English cars the company turned to the coach-building firms of Barker, Connaught, and Maythorne.

Bottom: 1926 Renault, front view, model unknown, Renault S.A., Paris. This illustration is by Raymond Loewy (1893-1986), who later became famous as an industrial designer, notably for the Pennsylvania Railroad and Studebaker. Renault achieved its unique streamlined styling by placing the radiator behind the engine and completely concealing it in the body work. The star above Renault's front diamond emblem indicates this car is in the prestige "Stella" class.

DIANA STRAIGHT "8"

WOLVERINE

LOEWY

PLATE 66

Top: 1927 Studebaker President Big Six, 75-hp Custom Sedan, priced at $2,245, The Studebaker Corporation of America, South Bend, IN.

Middle: 1926 Peerless Model Six-80, 6-cylinder, 68-hp Boattail Roadster, Peerless Motor Car Co. Cleveland, OH.

Bottom: 1927 Studebaker Standard Six, 50-hp Custom Victoria, priced at $1,335. In 1927, Studebaker introduced its figurative "Atalanta" ornament to replace the Boyce Moto-Meter mounted atop the radiator cap of its previous models. The Peerless shown here has a Boyce Moto-Meter, which had a thermometer indicating water temperature. In 1927, Peerless introduced an eagle-head radiator cap ornament.

S T U D E B A K E R

PLATE 67

Cars from 1927:

Top: Paige Six-45, 43-hp, 5-passenger Brougham, priced at $1,095, The Paige-Detroit Motor Car Co., Detroit, MI.

Upper middle left: Auburn Sedan, likely a Model 8-88, Auburn Automobile Co., Auburn, IN.

Middle right: Reo Flying Cloud, 6-cylinder, 65-hp, 2-door Brougham, priced at $2,300, Reo Motor Car Co., Lansing, MI.

Lower middle left: This Chrysler is likely the Series 70, 6-cylinder, 68-hp Roadster, Chrysler Corporation, Detroit, MI. Chrysler built 182,195 cars in 1927, ranking it seventh in the industry.

Bottom: Star Six, 40-hp Sedan, priced at $925, Durant Motors Inc., Elizabeth, NJ. This was the final year of production for this car as a Star. The following year it was marketed as the Durant Model 55.

PLATE 68

Top: 1928 Lincoln Model L, V-8, 90-hp Dietrich Convertible Sedan, Lincoln Motor Co., Detroit, MI.

Middle: 1927 Rolls-Royce Landaulet, Rolls-Royce Ltd., Derby, England.

Bottom: 1928 Pontiac, 6-cylinder, 48-hp Sport Landau Sedan, priced at $875, Oakland Motor Car Co., Pontiac, Michigan. General Motors' Pontiac originated in 1926 as a cheaper version of the Oakland, the original concept being a 6-cylinder motor mounted on a Chevrolet chassis built for a 4-cylinder motor. When Oakland was discontinued at the end of 1931, Pontiac continued on as Pontiac Motor Co., Pontiac, MI. Combined Pontiac/Oakland output for 1928 was 244,584 cars, placing it fifth in U.S. production. Variations of the Native American head-and-headdress was used as a logo (seen here as the hood ornament) until 1956, when it was updated to the Native American red arrowhead design.

PLATE 69

Cars from 1928:

Top: Stearns-Knight, 8-cylinder, 112-hp Coupe, priced at $5,500, F.B. Stearns Co., Cleveland. This firm offered America's only 8-cylinder Knight sleeve-valve motor. From December 1925 onward, it was a subsidiary of Willys-Overland, but it soon became a victim of the Great Depression, ceasing production on December 20, 1929, barely two months after the stock market crash.

Middle: Stearns-Knight Sedan (model unknown).

Bottom: Nash Standard Six, 45-hp, 2-door Sedan, priced at $1,000, Nash Motors Co., Kenosha, WI. Nash ranked eighth in U.S. auto production in 1928, building 138,137 cars.

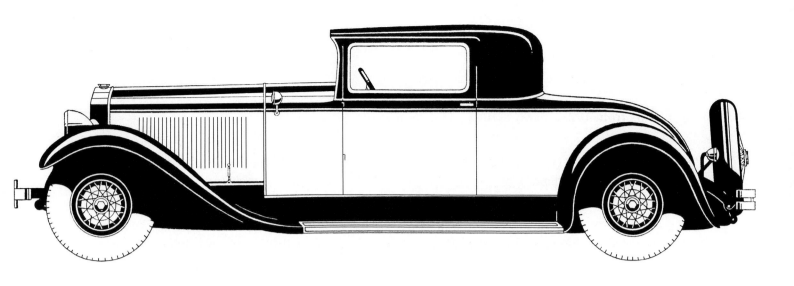

STEARNS·KNIGHT

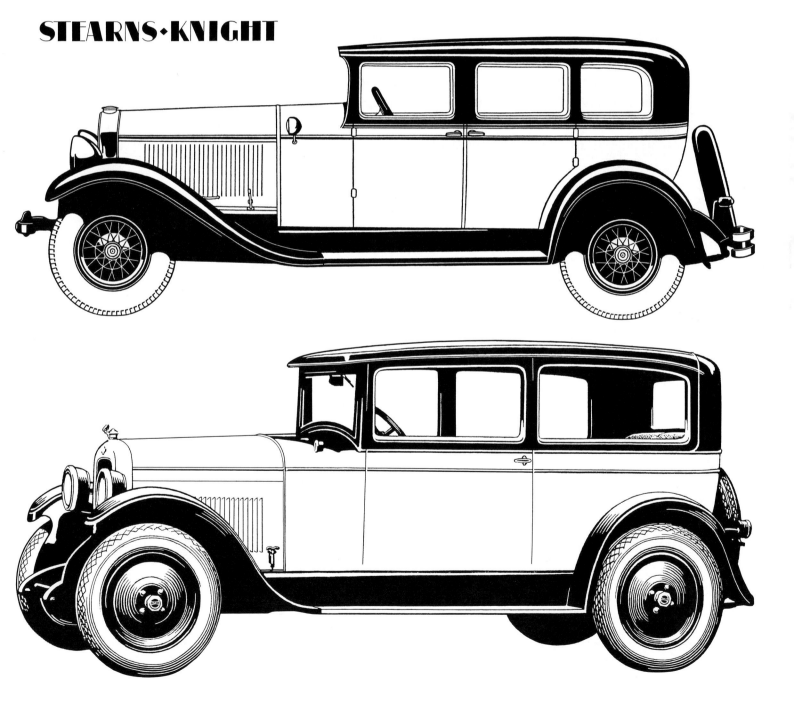

PLATE 70

Cars from 1928:

Top: Rolls-Royce car, perhaps the Gurney Nutting Weyman Saloon model, Rolls-Royce Ltd., Derby, England.

Middle right: Dodge Brothers Senior Six, 68-hp Cabriolet, English version with rumble seat, Dodge Brothers, Detroit, MI. The American price of this car was $1,595. This same year the company was sold to Chrysler Corporation, and from about 1930 onwards the car was simply known as the Dodge.

Bottom: Bentley car (model unknown), Bentley Motors, Ltd., Crewe, England. Bentley was founded by W.O. Bentley, who during World War I was involved in aircraft engine manufacture. His first car, which featured a 3-liter, 4-cylinder engine with overhead-camshaft, was designed in 1919 but wasn't sold until 1921. The car shown here likely has the 4.5 liter, 6-cylinder, 110-hp engine. Bentley racers won at Le Mans from 1927 to 1930, but despite this the company failed in 1931, thereafter becoming a subsidiary of Rolls-Royce.

BM 1928

PLATE 71

Top: 1929 DeSoto Model K, 6-cylinder, 55-hp Deluxe Sedan, priced at $955, DeSoto Motor Corporation, Detroit, MI. Chrysler Corporation's DeSoto was unveiled in mid-1928 for the 1929 model year, selling 81,065 cars in 12 months. This set an initial production record that lasted until 1960 when the Ford Falcon was introduced. One of Chrysler Corporation's styling innovations was the thin-profile radiator which can be seen in this picture.

Middle: 1928 Franklin air-cooled Airman Series, 6-cylinder, 46-hp Coupe, priced at $2,490, Franklin Automobile Co., Syracuse, NY.

Bottom: 1928 Marmon Straight Eight Sedan, English version, Nordyke & Marmon Co., Indianapolis, IN. At this time Marmon 8-cylinder sedans were offered in 42- and 86-hp versions.

PLATE 72

Cars from 1929:

Top: Chrysler Series 80 L, 6-cylinder, 110-hp Imperial Roadster with rumble seat, priced at $2,895, Chrysler Corporation, Detroit, MI.

Middle: Plymouth 4-cylinder, 45-hp Roadster with rumble seat, priced at $675, Chrysler Corporation, Detroit, MI. Plymouth was Chrysler's entry into the low price market where it was primarily competing with Ford and Chevrolet. Its engine was a further development of one that Chrysler had inherited from Maxwell.

Bottom: Pierce-Arrow Model 126, 8-cylinder, 125-hp Convertible Coupe with rumble seat, The Pierce-Arrow Motor Car Co., Buffalo, NY.

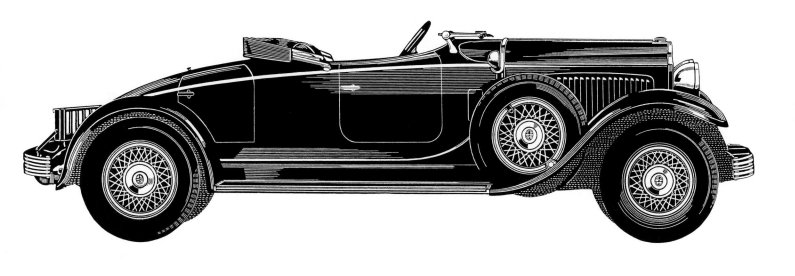

PLATE 73

Cars from 1929:

Top: Oldsmobile Model F-29, 6-cylinder, 62-hp Convertible Coupe, Olds Motor Works, Lansing, MI.

Middle: Oldsmobile Model F-29, 6-cylinder, 62-hp, 4-door Sedan.

Bottom: Vauxhall 20-60, 6-cylinder, 2.9 litre Velox Saloon., Vauxhall Motors, Luton, England. The company began in 1857 as a pump and marine engine manufacturer. It began car production in 1903, and was purchased by General Motors Corporation in 1925.

PLATE 74

Cars from 1929:

Top: Pontiac Six, 60-hp, 2-door Sedan, priced at $745, Oakland Motor Co., Pontiac, MI.

Middle: Oakland 6-cylinder, 2-door Sedan, priced at $1,145, Oakland Motor Co., Pontiac, MI. Combined Pontiac/Oakland production that year was 211,054 cars, placing it fifth in the industry.

Bottom: Buick Series 116, Model 20, 6-cylinder, 94-hp, 2-door Sedan, Buick Motor Co., Flint, MI. Buick ranked sixth in U.S. auto production, with 196,104 cars.

PLATE 75

Top: 1930 Chrysler 77, 6-cylinder, 93-hp, 4-door Royal Sedan, priced at $1,775, Chrysler Corporation, Detroit, MI. Chrysler placed eighth in industry production that year, building 77,881 cars.

Middle Left: 1930 6-cylinder Chevrolet (model unknown), Chevrolet Motor Co., Detroit, MI. Chevrolet built 640,980 vehicles that year, ranking it second in the industry.

Upper middle right: 1930 Marquette Model 37, 6-cylinder, 67-hp, 4-door Sedan, Buick Motor Co., Flint, MI. The Marquette was a companion brand to Buick, like LaSalle was to Cadillac, and Pontiac to Oakland. Although well built, its introduction coincided with the beginning of the Great Depression, and it quickly fell victim.

Lower middle right: 1929 Essex, 6-cylinder, 4-door Sedan, priced at $795, Hudson Motor Car Co., Detroit, MI. Combined Hudson/Essex output in 1929 was 300,962 cars, placing it third in U.S. production.

Bottom: 1930 Chrysler 70, 6-cylinder, 75-hp Royal Coupe with rumble seat, priced at $1,345.

PLATE 76

Cars from 1930:

Top: DeSoto Model CF, 8-cylinder, 70-hp Roadster, priced at $965, DeSoto Motor Corporation, Detroit, MI.

Middle. A 4-door Nash sedan from the "400" series, likely the Model 494, 7-passenger Sedan with a straight-8, 100-hp engine, priced at $2,085, Nash Motors Co., Kenosha, WI.

Bottom: DeSoto Model CF, 8-cylinder, 70-hp Convertible Coupe.

1930
NASH
"400"

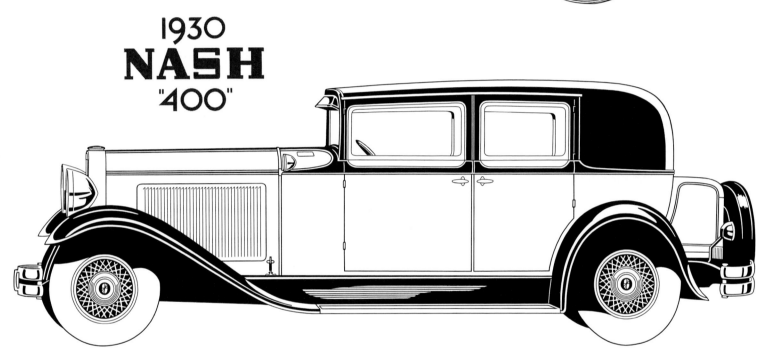

AUTOMOBILE IMAGE SOURCES

Atlantic Monthly, Boston

Arts & Decoration, New York

Automobile Topics Illustrated, New York

Colliers: The National Weekly, New York

Country Gentleman, Curtis Publishing Co., Philadelphia

Country Life in America, Doubleday, Page & Co., Garden City, NY

Cycle & Automobile Trade Journal, Chilton Co., Philadelphia

Engineering News & American Railway Journal, Sep. 8, 1888. New York

Farm & Ranch, Dallas

Farm Implement News, Chicago

Farm Life, Farm Life Publishing Co., Spencer, IN

Harper's Bazar, Harper & Brothers, New York

The Horseless Age, The Horseless Age Co., New York

House & Garden, Conde Nast Publications, New York

Illustrated London News, London

Implement & Vehicle Journal, Dallas

La Nature: Revue des Sciences, G. Masson, Paris

La Revue Scientifique et Industrielle de l'Annee (1898), Hachette, Paris

Laverne, Gerard, *The Automobile: Its Construction & Management*, Cassell & Co. Ltd., London, 1902

Loewy Design LLC / www.RaymondLoewy.com

Life, New York

L'Illustration, Paris

McClure's Magazine, S.S. McClure Co., New York

Meyers Groses Konversations - Lexicon, Band 14, Leipzig, 1908

Motor, Hearst Publications, New York

Motor Age, Class Journal Co., Chicago

Motor Life, Frederick Marriott, San Francisco

Munsey's Magazine, Frank A. Munsey Co., New York

National Geographic Magazine, National Geographic Society, Washington, DC

Outlook, New York

Progressive Farmer, Dallas

Punch, or the London Charivari, London

Review of Reviews, New York

Saturday Evening Post, Curtis Publishing Co., Philadelphia

St. Louis Globe-Democrat, St. Louis

Sunset Magazine, San Francisco

The American Magazine, Phillips Publishing Co., New York

The Autocar, Iliffe & Sons, Ltd. London

The Automobile Magazine, New York

The Automobile Trade Journal, Chilton Co., Philadelphia

The Engineer, London

The Independent Magazine, New York

The Literary Digest, Funk & Wagnalls, New York

The Rural New-Yorker: A Journal for the Suburban & Country Home, The Rand Publishing Co., New York

BIBLIOGRAPHY

"American Self-Propelled Carriages," *The Engineer* Volume LXXXI, London, January 3, 1896.

Bailey, L. Scott, *World of Cars*, Automobile Quarterly, Inc., New York, 1971.

Baxter, William Jr. "The Evolution and Present Status of the Automobile," *Popular Science Monthly* Volume 57, D. Appleton & Co., New York, August 1900.

Berkebile, Don H., *The 1893 Duryea Automobile*, Smithsonian Institution, Washington, DC., 1964.

Bowman, Richard, *Maxwell: First Builder of Chrysler Cars*, http://www.allpar.com/history/maxwell.html

Brooks, John, "A Corner in Stutz," *The New Yorker*, New York, Aug. 23, 1969.

Clymer, Floyd, *Those Wonderful Old Automobiles*, Bonanza Books, New York, 1953.

Cobb, Harold M., *The History of Stainless Steel*, ASM International, Materials Park, Ohio, 2010.

Curcio, Vincent, *Chrysler: The Life and Times of an Automotive Genius*, Oxford University Press, Oxford & New York, 2000.

Encyclopedia of American Coachbuilders & Coachbuilding, www.coachbuilt.com

Harter, Jim, *World Railways of the Nineteenth Century: A Pictorial History in Victorian Engravings*, Johns Hopkins University Press, Baltimore & London, 2005.

Hebb, David, *Wheels on the Road: A History of the Automobile from the Steam Engine to the Car of Tomorrow*, Collier Books, New York, 1966.

Flammang, James M., *Chronicle of the American Automobile: Over 100 Years of Auto History*, Publications International, Ltd., Lincolnwood, Illinois, 1994.

Fletcher, William, *English & American Steam Carriages and Traction Engines*, David & Charles (Holdings) Ltd., London, 1973.

Kimes, Beverly Rae & Clark, Henry Austin Jr., *Standard Catalog of American Cars: 1805-1942*, Krause Publications, Iola, Wisconsin. 1985.

McAuliffe, Mary, *Twilight of the Belle Epoque*, Rowman & Littlefield, Lanham, Maryland, 2014.

Moorhouse, Robert, *The Illustrated History of Tractors*, Chartwell Books, Edison, New Jersey, 1996.

"New Steam Carriage," *Scientific American*, New York, Nov. 28, 1863.

Rae, John B., *The American Automobile: A Brief History*, The University of Chicago Press, Chicago, 1965.

Roberts, Peter, *Collectors History of the Automobile: The Development of Man's Greatest Means of Transportation*, Bonanza Books, New York, 1978.

Russell, Jesse & Cohn, Ronald, *Effects of the Automobile on Societies*, Bookvika/Lennex Corporation, Edinburgh, 2012.

Sears, Stephen W., *The Automobile in America*, American Heritage Publishing Co., New York, 1977.

Wallis, Michael & Williamson, Michael S., *The Lincoln Highway: Coast to Coast from Times Square to the Golden Gate*, W.W. Norton & Co., New York, 2007.

Wikipedia: The Free Encyclopedia

Wise, David Burgess, *The Motor Car: An Illustrated International History*, G.P. Putnam's Sons, New York, 1979.

Index

Published Works by Jim Harter

Early Farm Tractors: A History in Advertising Line Art, Wings Press, San Antonio, 2013.

Scientific Instruments and Apparatus: CD-ROM and Book, Dover Publications, Mineola, NY, 2007.

Insects: CD-ROM and Book, Dover Publications, Mineola, NY, 2007.

World Railways of the Nineteenth Century: A Pictorial History in Victorian Engravings, The Johns Hopkins University Press, Baltimore, 2005.

Nautical Illustrations: 681 Permission-free Illustrations from Nineteenth Century Sources, Dover Publications, Mineola, NY, 2003.

Initiations in the Abyss: A Surrealist Apocalypse, Wings Press, San Antonio, 2003.

Landscapes and Cityscapes for Artists and Craftspeople: From 19th-Century Sources, Dover Publications, Mineola, NY, 1999.

American Railroads of the Nineteenth Century: A Pictorial History in Victorian Wood Engravings, Texas Tech University Press, Lubbock, 1998.

The Ultimate Angel Book, Gramercy Books, New York, 1995.

Images of Medicine, Bonanza Books, New York, 1991.

Images of World Architecture, Bonanza Books, New York, 1990.

The Plant Kingdom Compendium, Bonanza Books, New York, 1988.

Journeys in the Mythic Sea: An Innerspace Odyssey, Harmony Books, New York, 1985.

Hands: A Pictorial Archive from Nineteenth Century Sources, Dover Publications, New York, 1985.

Transportation: A Pictorial Archive from Nineteenth Century Sources, Dover Publications, New York, 1984.

Music: A Pictorial Archive of Woodcuts and Engravings, Dover Publications, New York, 1980.

Men: A Pictorial Archive from Nineteenth Century Sources, Dover Publications, New York, 1980.

Animals: A Pictorial Archive from Nineteenth Century Sources, Dover Publications, New York, 1980.

Food and Drink: A Pictorial Archive from Nineteenth Century Sources, Dover Publications, New York, 1979.

Women: A Pictorial Archive from Nineteenth Century Sources, Dover Publications, New York, 1978.

Harter's Picture Archive for Collage and Illustrations, Dover Publications, New York, 1978.

Die Gretchen, Speleo Press, Austin, 1973.

About the Author

━━━ 215 ━━━

B orn on Oct. 2, 1941, in Lubbock, Texas, Jim Harter was largely self-taught as an artist. From 1969 to 1972 he played a small part in creating posters for Austin's legendary rock venues, the Vulcan Gas Company and Armadillo World Headquarters. Influenced by San Francisco collage artist Wilfried Satty, Harter turned to making surrealist collages from 19th century engravings. In 1976 he moved to New York, becoming a freelance illustrator, and editor of clip-art books for Dover, and later for other publications. Since then, two books of his collages, *Journeys in the Mythic Sea* and *Initiations in the Abyss* have been published, as well as two railroad history books illustrated entirely with Victorian engravings. In 1984, he began painting using an old-master technique, under the guidance of Carlos Madrid. This work was influenced by his earlier collages, but also owes something to Symbolism, Surrealism, Fantastic Realism, and an exposure to Eastern Philosophy. During the early 1980s Harter became friends with Dr. Jean Letschert, a Belgian visionary painter and former student of Rene Magritte. He also met members of Holland's Metarealist group, and fantastic realist painters in New York. In 1986, Harter moved to San Antonio, Texas where he remains today. In recent years he has returned to his collage work, digitally colorizing a number of his creations.

Wings Press was founded in 1975 by Joanie Whitebird and Joseph F. Lomax, both deceased, as "an informal association of artists and cultural mythologists dedicated to the preservation of the literature of the nation of Texas." Publisher, editor and designer since 1995, Bryce Milligan is honored to carry on and expand that mission to include the finest in American writing—meaning all of the Americas, without commercial considerations clouding the decision to publish or not to publish.

Wings Press intends to produce multi-cultural books, chapbooks, ebooks, recordings and broadsides that enlighten the human spirit and enliven the mind. Everyone ever associated with Wings has been or is a writer, and we know well that writing is a transformational art form capable of changing the world, primarily by allowing us to glimpse something of each other's souls. We believe that good writing is innovative, insightful, and interesting. But most of all it is honest. As Bob Dylan put it, "To live outside the law, you must be honest."

Likewise, Wings Press is committed to treating the planet itself as a partner. Thus the press uses as much recycled material as possible, from the paper on which the books are printed to the boxes in which they are shipped.

As Robert Dana wrote in *Against the Grain,* "Small press publishing is personal publishing. In essence, it's a matter of personal vision, personal taste and courage, and personal friendships." Welcome to our world.

Colophon

This first edition of *Early Automobiles: A History in Advertising Line Art*, by Jim Harter, has been printed on 70 pound Edwards Brothers Matte Coated Paper containing a percentage of recycled fiber. Titles have been set in Colonna MT and Warnock Pro type, the text in Adobe Caslon type. All Wings Press books are designed and produced by Bryce Milligan.

On-line catalogue and ordering available at
www.wingspress.com

Wings Press titles are distributed to the
trade by the
Independent Publishers Group
www.ipgbook.com

Also available as an ebook.